WAGONS OF THE EARLY BRITISH RAIL ERA

A Pictorial Study of the 1969 to 1982 Period

WAGONS OF THE EARLY BRITISH RAIL ERA

A Pictorial Study of the 1969 to 1982 Period

David Larkin

WAGONS OF THE EARLY BRITISH RAIL ERA

Kestrel Railway Books
PO Box 269
SOUTHAMPTON
SO30 4XR

www.kestrelrailwaybooks.co.uk

Printed by the Amadeus Press.

ISBN 978-1-905505-10-4

Front cover (top left): VBB 200112 as original with new code at Battersea in August 1976. (Author's Ref No W6573/DL)
Front cover (bottom left): 25T Lowmac as RRV B904511 at Portsmouth in February 1980. (Author's Ref No W10056/DL)
Front cover (top right): COAL 21 B316477 as new at Swansea Docks in April 1975. (Author's Ref No W4897/DL)
Front cover (bottom right): BEV temporary coil wagon B923566 at Rochester in April 1980. (Author's Ref No W8808/DL)

Back cover (top left): BOV Bogie Pipe Wagon B924480 at Rochester in October 1978. (Author's Ref No W7077/DL)
Back cover (top right): VCA 200352 with maroon livery at Brixton in March 1979. (Author's Ref No W6506/DL)
Back cover (bottom left): FWV Boflat B947908 at Swansea Docks in August 1981. (Author's Ref No W9187/DL)
Back cover (bottom right): Carflat B745154 with export cars at Battersea in October 1976. (Author's Ref No W7471/DL)

Contents

Introduction vii

Wagon Number Series Details 1

Wagon Diagram Numbers and TOPS Codes 2

Wagon Liveries and Lettering 6

Wagon Descriptions
    Rebuilt 16T Mineral Wagons (Unfitted) 9
    Rebuilt 16T Mineral Wagons (Vacuum braked, 9ft wheelbase) 11
    Rebuilt 16T Mineral Wagons (Vacuum braked, 10ft wheelbase) 13
    Rebuilt 21T Mineral Wagons (Unfitted, 1975–76 rebuilds) 15
    Rebuilt 21T Mineral Wagons (1977–78 rebuilds) 17
    Rebuilt 21T Coal Hopper Wagons (1971–78 rebuilds) 20
    Carflats and MTV Sand Wagons 31
    COIL S (KSV) Wagons 33
    COIL R (KRV) Wagons 35
    COIL E (KEV) Wagons 37
    Steel-carrying Wagons (Strip Coil Conversions) 39
    Bogie Pipe-carrying Wagons 41
    Barrier Wagons (RBV) 43
    Runner Wagons (RRO, RRV) 45
    Air-braked Open Wagons (OAA) 47
    Air-braked Open Wagons (OBA) 49
    Air-braked Vans (Early Batches, VAB/VBB) 51
    Air-braked Vans (VCA) 55
    Air-braked Vans (VDA) 57
    Air-braked Covered Hopper Wagons (CBA) 59
    Air-braked Hopper Wagons (HAA) 60
    Air-braked Hopper Wagons (HBA) 61
    Air-braked 4-wheel Steel-carrying Wagons (SAA, SAB) 63
    Air-braked 4-wheel Steel-carrying Wagons (SPA) 65
    Air-braked Flask Wagons (XKA, XKB) 67
    Air-braked Bogie Steel-carrying Wagons (BAA, BAB) 69
    Air-braked Bogie Steel-carrying Wagons (BBA) 71
    Air-braked Bogie Steel-carrying Wagons (BDA) 73
    Air-braked Bogie Steel-carrying Wagons (BPA, BRA, XVA) 75
    Air-braked Miscellaneous Wagons (BCA, BLA, FMA, KOA, KTA) 77
    Air-braked Miscellaneous Wagons (MFA and WR Test Train) 81
    Boplate E Conflat Conversions 85
    Summary of Period 1st January 1969 to 31st December 1982 87

B923715 taken at Longport, Staffordshire in August 1980. The changing of codes on the TOPS computer was effected far more quickly than the painted code, but these were done when convenient. It appears that chalked codes were applied to help the painters, as with the wagon on the right. (Author's Ref No W8924B/DL)

Opposite page: B596389 at Hoo Junction, Rochester in August 1980. The rebodying of a vast fleet of 16T Mineral wagons was dubious and the conversion of Palbrick wagons even more eccentric. This particular wagon is thus one of the very few MCV wagons to have roller bearings; it is also 10ft wheelbase of course. (Author's Ref No W8472/DL)

Introduction

Although British Rail had technically come into being a few years early, I have chosen 1969 as the starting point as it was the first full year of non-steam operation. Freight train matters in fact showed little change and it was easy to regularly photograph pre-Nationalisation wagons and vans, albeit of the vacuum-braked, 10ft wheelbase types or specialist vehicles.

1969 was also the year that large numbers of mineral and hopper coal-carrying wagons began to be rebodied totally, rather than just being patched up. Initially this involved only 16T Minerals but later included all the other capacities as well.

At the same time, orders were placed for the first air-braked general purpose open and van designs, which were relatively successful: a Covhop variant of the Hop AB and a four-wheeled steel carrier, which was very short-lived in its designed role.

A major step forward was the introduction of the TOPS computerised wagon record system in 1972. This greatly simplified wagon codes to three letters and, more to the point, enabled each wagon, including privately owned and departmental stock, to be tracked and correctly utilised.

Vacuum-braked wagons were only built in small numbers and involved conversions. Approximately 250 further Carflat wagons were produced together with 150 sand wagons. Some vacuum-braked 10ft wheelbase 16T Minerals were built using ex-Palbrick chassis but most of the "new" Mineral and Hopper wagons were unfitted.

Further air-braked designs appeared, including open wagons, vans, plate wagons, domestic coal hoppers and others. Bogie steel wagons were a mixture of new designs and conversions.

Finally, the air-braked fleet was separated from the other wagons by brand name, firstly by code, ABN (for Air Braked Network), and then by name, Railfreight, and with new liveries. Compatible privately-owned wagons operated with BR–owned stock on a pattern of set routes, echoing the old Condor and Speedlink services and on a par with Freightliner services

The acknowledgements from the earlier volumes are repeated, especially to Jean.

David Larkin,
May 2009

Other Books in this Series

Volume 1: Wagons of the Early British Railways Era – A Pictorial Study of the 1948 to 1954 Period

David Larkin is well-known for his study of British Railways goods wagons, and this book pays particular attention to those ordered by BR in the earliest years of its existence. The "Big Four" pre-nationalisation companies all had outstanding wagon orders under construction in 1948, and these continued to be delivered with their original numbers, albeit with new prefix letters.

In addition, the newly-created BR acquired a fleet of wagons from the erstwhile Ministry of War Transport. These are also considered in this book, together with the early BR orders for wagons based on the "Big Four" designs and on its own early standard designs in the period up to the eve of the "Modernisation Plan" of 1955.

Profusely illustrated, this book includes lot and diagram details, wagon number ranges, builders' and livery details of vehicles as diverse as Lowfit wagons, open wagons, containers and container wagons, mineral wagons, ventilated vans, railtanks, cattle wagons and brake vans.

ISBN: 978-0-9544859-8-6

Volume 2: Wagons of the Middle British Railways Era – A Pictorial Study of the 1955 to 1961 Period

In this volume David Larkin continues to use his of knowledge of British Railways goods wagons to review the middle years of BR, and this book pays particular attention to the vast numbers of wagons inspired by the Ideal Stocks Committee and built under the 1955 Modernisation Scheme.

Profusely illustrated, this book includes all the usual lot and diagram details, wagon number ranges, builder's and livery details and lists at some length the route lettering carried by these vehicles. The final examples of such types as single bolsters, banana vans and ventilated fruit vans are covered, as is the emergence of new types like the Presflo and Covhop.

ISBN: 978-1-905505-06-7

Volume 3: Wagons of the Final Years of British Railways – A Pictorial Study of the 1962 to 1968 Period

In this volume David Larkin looks at the final flowering of vacuum-braked stock, and the development of air-braked stock in the final years of British Railways, such as "merry-go-round" coal hoppers and Freightliner flat wagons. The batch of vacuum-fitted prototypes that eventually led to the general fleet of air-braked opens and vans is also covered. In addition, David also considers the effect of the change of corporate image for British Rail on wagon liveries, as a prelude to his continuation of the series into the British Rail era.

Profusely illustrated, this book includes lot and diagram details, wagon number ranges, builder's and livery details of a diverse set of vehicles.

ISBN: 978-1-905505-08-1

Other volumes planned are:

Volume 5: Wagons of the Later British Rail Era – A Pictorial Study of the 1983 to 1994 Period

This volume covers the final new air-braked stock, the conversions and new liveries, taking the story up to Privatisation.

Volume 6: Ballast Wagons of British Railways – A Pictorial Study of the Engineers Wagon Fleet from 1948 Onwards

This volume covers the various fish-named vehicles (such as CATFISH, DOGFISH, GRAMPUS and SHARK) in depth.

Wagon Number Series

Wagon Number Series (Traditional Fleet)

The following list reiterates previous notes and adds the last number ranges issued after 1968.

B596000 to B596393	16T Mineral Wagons, rebodied vehicles on 10ft wheelbase vacuum-braked chassis.
B315000 to B317599	21T Mineral NF Wagons, rebodied vehicles on various chassis.
B290000 to B290485	25Tonne Mineral Wagons, rebodied vehicles on various chassis (not all built).
B340000 to B340924	25Tonne Hopper VB Wagons, rebodied vehicles on various chassis (not all built).
B345000 to B346468	25Tonne Hopper NF Wagons, rebodied vehicles on various chassis (not all built).
B350000 to B355796	26T/32T Hopper AB Wagons, "merry-go-round" wagons, B-prefix dropped after this and continued in Air-braked series.
B531000 to B531007	38T Rectank Wagons, reclassified as Conflat.
B390000 to B390149	21T Sand Wagons.
B745000 to B745302	Car-carrying Wagons.
B960000 to B960023	COIL X wagons (COIL X conversions).

Wagon Number Series (Air-braked Fleet)

100000 to 113049	Open Wagons (with gaps, see text).
150000 to 150004	Platform wagons.
200000 to 230549	Vans (with gaps, see text).
250000 to 250056, 375000 to 375137	Covered Hoppers.
350000 to 359571, 360000 to 361998, 365000 to 366129, 368000 to 368459	Coal Hoppers.
390000 to 390001, 391000 to 391046, 470000 to 470180	Mineral Wagons.
400000 to 400299, 460000 to 461101	4-wheeled Steel.
550000 to 550050	Nuclear Flask.
900000 to 990049	Bogie Steel (with gaps, see text).

Wagon Diagram Numbers and TOPS Codes

The introduction in 1972 of the computerised Total Operating Processing System (TOPS) had great implications for the whole working of British Rail and moved it into the 20th Century. As far as wagons were concerned, each wagon was given a new "Design Code" rather than a diagram number, for example HA001C in place of diagram 1/156 for the prototype HOP AB, B350000. The first two letters became the first two letters of the painted code, "HA" and the third letter was the brake type, thus HAA in this case. The following table lists alphabetically the painted codes that were issued. Please note that very few pre-BR wagons were ever so coded, although computerised records show that design codes, and indeed new diagrams, were produced for them.

BAA:	Air-braked 900049 – 900198 and 900200 – 900305 (many recoded).
BAB:	Air-braked 900000 – 900048 (many recoded).
BBA:	Air-braked 910000 – 910120, 910161 to 910365, 910367 – 910591 (many recoded).
BCA:	Air-braked 960000 – 960001 (code not used after 1980, vehicles transferred).
BCO:	Non-fitted Bogie Bolster C wagons (B922000 – 499, B940000 – 999, B943000 – 5790).
BCV:	Vacuum-braked Bogie Bolster C (B922500 – 3299, B924400 – 799, B945791 – 990).
BCW:	Dual-braked conversion of BCV.
BDA:	Air-braked 950000 – 951250 (many recoded).
BDO:	Non-fitted Bogie Bolster D wagons (B941000 – B942929, B927000 – B927399).
BDV:	Vacuum-braked Bogie Bolster D wagons (B927400 – B928199) (some recoded).
BDW:	Dual-braked conversion of BDV.
BEA:	
BEV:	Vacuum-braked Bogie Bolster E wagons (B923300 – 499, B924800 – 99) (many recoded).
BFA:	Re-rated air-braked BDA wagons.
BGA:	Air-braked 961000 – 961003.
BHA:	Air-braked 962000 – 962003.
BHV:	Converted BCV wagons with higher stanchions (some recoded).
BHW:	Dual-braked conversion of BHV.
BJA:	Air-braked 963000 – 963003.
BKA:	Converted BAA wagons with coil cradles (some recoded).
BKB:	Converted BAB wagons with coil cradles (some recoded).
BLA:	Air-braked 920000 (code not used after 1979, vehicle transferred).
BMA:	Converted BPA wagons.
BOA:	Air-braked 990000 – 990049 (some recoded).
BOV:	Converted BCV wagons with tall tube cradles.
BPA:	Air-braked 965000 – 965079 (some recoded).
BPO:	Non-fitted BOPLATE E wagons (B947000 – B947859).
BPV:	Vacuum-braked BOPLATE E wagons (B947860 – 8409) (many recoded).
BQV:	Converted BCV and BHV wagons to carry large diameter gas pipes.
BQW:	Dual-braked conversion of BQV.
BRA:	Air-braked 967500 – 967649 (some recoded).
BRP:	Vacuum-piped BORAIL wagons (B946050 – B946064).
BRV:	Vacuum-braked BORAIL wagons (B946065 – B946229) (many recoded).
BTA:	Converted BDA wagons to carry logs.
BTV:	Converted BCV wagons to carry logs.
BTW:	Dual-braked conversion of BTV
BUA:	Converted BBA to carry hot coil.
BYA:	Converted BAA.
BZA:	Converted BAA.
CAO:	Non-fitted Brake Vans.
CAP:	Vacuum-piped Brake Vans.
CAR:	Air-piped and Vacuum-piped Brake Vans (B954/B955XXX series, see text).
CBA:	Air-braked 250000 – 250056.

CCO: CHO wagons allocated to sand traffic.
CCP: CHP wagons allocated to sand traffic.
CCV: CHP wagons allocated to sand traffic.
CDA: Air-braked 375000 – 375137.
CGO: Non-fitted Bulk Grain wagons (B885000 – B885509).
CGP: Vacuum-piped Bulk Grain wagons (B885610 – B885709) (some recoded).
CGV: Vacuum-braked Bulk Grain wagons (B885510 – B885609).
CHO: Non-fitted COVHOP wagons (B886000 – B886561) (some recoded).
CHP: Vacuum-piped COVHOP wagons (B870500 – 759, B886562 – 996) (some recoded).
CHV: Vacuum-braked COVHOP wagons (B870760 – 879) (some recoded).
CPV: Vacuum-braked PRESFLO wagons (B873024 – 193, B873200 – 369, B873420 – 719, B887800 – B888980) (see CPW entry).
CPW: Dual-braked PRESFLO wagons (B887811, plus at least 105 others).
CQV: Vacuum-braked PRESTWIN wagons (B873000 – 23, B873194 – 9, B873370 – 419).
CSA: Air-braked FLY ASH wagons (B873978 – B874185).
CSV: Vacuum-braked FLY ASH wagons (B873771 – 93, B873894 – 977).
CXV: Vacuum-braked Gunpowder vans (various numbers).
CZP: Vacuum-piped CHP wagons converted for sugar.
CZV: Vacuum-braked CHV wagons converted for sugar.
FAV: Vacuum-braked CONFLAT A wagons.
FBB: Air-braked 511000 – 5511022.
FEV: Converted BPV wagons to carry containers.
FFA: Air-braked FREIGHTLINER inner wagons.
FGA: Air-braked FREIGHTLINER outer wagons.
FGB: Dual-braked FREIGHTLINER outer wagons.
FHA: Air-braked 699000 – 699003.
FIA: Possibly used on RIV wagons.
FIX: Dual-braked CAR C wagons (21 70 414 0 xxx-x range).
FLV: Vacuum-braked CONFLAT L wagons.
FMA: Air-braked FREIGHTFLAT wagons (converted FFA/FGA to carry vehicles).
FVA: Air-braked CARFLAT wagons.
FVV: Vacuum-braked CARFLAT wagons.
FVX: Dual-braked CARFLAT wagons.
FWV: Vacuum-braked BPV wagons to carry coil/car traffic.
FZA: Air-braked 150000 – 150004.
HAA: Air-braked MGR coal hoppers (HOP AB).
HBA: Air-braked 360000 – 361998 (modified and code changed to HEA).
HCA: Air-braked MGR coal hoppers (HOP 32 AB) (late coding).
HCO: Non-fitted Coke Hoppers (B447000 – 8649, B448900 – 9199).
HCP: Vacuum-piped Coke Hoppers (B448650 – 899).
HDA: Air-braked MGR coal hoppers (368000 – 368459).
HEA: Re-sprung HBA wagons (some recoded).
HIO: Erroneous use for HJO and HKO wagons.
HJO: Non-fitted Iron-ore Hopper Wagons (B438000 – B440049, with gaps).
HJV: Vacuum-braked HJO wagons.
HKV: Vacuum-braked Iron Ore Hopper Wagons (B437500 – 999, B445150 – 419).
HTO: Non-fitted 21T Coal Hopper Wagons (B345000 – 6468, plus many others).
HTP: Vacuum-piped 21T Coal Hopper Wagons (some B-prefixed numbers).
HTV: Vacuum-braked 21T Coal Hopper Wagons (B340000 – 924, plus other B-prefixed).
HUO: Non-fitted 24 1/2T Coal Hopper Wagons (B333000 – 8262).
IOX: Erroneous use for OIX wagons.
JAV: Vacuum-braked Bogie Strip Coil wagons (B949000 – B949049).

JEV:	Vacuum-braked Bogie Strip Coil wagons (W16xxxx series).
JGV:	Vacuum-braked Bogie Strip Coil wagons (W16xxxx series).
JKX:	Dual-braked Bogie Strip Coil wagons (26 70 428 8 xxx-x series).
JMV:	Converted BDV wagons for strip coil.
JPV:	Converted BEV wagons for strip coil.
JRV:	Converted BEV wagons for strip coil.
JSV:	Converted BEV wagon for strip coil.
JTV:	Vacuum-braked Bogie Strip Coil wagon (B9495xx series).
JUV:	Converted BEV wagons for hot rolled coil.
JVV:	Vacuum-braked Bogie Strip Coil wagons (B949050 – B949089).
JWV:	Vacuum-braked Bogie Strip Coil Wagons (B949090 – B949129).
JXO:	Non-fitted Bogie Strip Coil wagons (B960000 – B960023).
JYV:	Converted BDV wagons for hot rolled coil.
JZV:	Vacuum-braked Bogie Strip Coil wagons (B949551 – B949608).
KAV:	Vacuum-braked Strip Coil wagons (B949130 – B949179).
KBV:	Vacuum-braked Strip Coil wagons (B949180 – B949219).
KCO:	Non-fitted Pig Iron wagons for strip coil.
KEV:	Converted SPV wagons for rod coil.
KGO:	Non-fitted Hot Pig Iron wagons for strip coil.
KHO:	Non-fitted Hot Pig Iron wagons for strip coil.
KJO:	Converted MSO wagons for strip coil.
KLV:	Converted OUV wagons for strip coil.
KOA:	Converted SAA wagons for rod coil.
KRV:	Converted SPV wagons for rod coil.
KSV:	Converted OWV wagons for rod coil.
KYV:	Converted OHV & OWV wagons for strip coil.
MAA:	Converted HAA wagons for mineral traffic.
MCO:	Non-fitted 16T Mineral wagons.
MCV:	Vacuum-braked 16T Mineral wagons.
MDO:	Non-fitted 21T Mineral wagons (B200000 – 2499, with gaps, B28xxxx series rebuilds, B290000 – 485, B315000 – 7599).
MDV:	Vacuum-braked 21T Mineral wagons (B290200 – 14, with gaps, B310000 – 4999).
MEA:	Converted HEA wagons for mineral traffic.
MEO:	Non-fitted 24 1/2 T Mineral wagons (B28xxxx series not rebuilt).
MFB:	Dual-braked 390000 – 390001.
MSO:	Non-fitted 27T Iron Ore Tippler wagons (B380000 – 8089, with gaps).
MSV:	Vacuum-braked 26T Iron Ore Tippler wagons (B385640 – 7089, B388090 – 9089).
MTV:	Vacuum-braked 23T Sand wagons (B390000 – B390149).
OAA:	Air-braked 100000 – 100099 (some recoded).
OBA:	Air-braked 110000 – 110800 (many recoded).
OCA:	Air-braked 112000 – 112399 (many recoded).
ODA:	Air-braked 113000 – 113049 (some recoded).
OHB:	Dual-braked OHV wagons (small number only).
OHV:	Vacuum-braked all-steel 13T Highfit wagons.
OIX:	Dual-braked Open wagons (B715000 – 39 & 21 70 619 0 xxx-x ranges).
OLV:	Vacuum-braked 13T Lowfit wagons.
OUV:	Vacuum-braked SHOCHOOD B wagons (B726225 – 524, with gaps).
OVV:	Vacuum-braked SHOCROOF A wagons (B726125 – 224).
OWV:	Vacuum-braked wooden & wood/steel 13T Highfit wagons.
RBA:	Air-braked Barrier wagons (various types).
RBB:	Dual-braked Barrier wagons (various types).
RBV:	Vacuum-braked Barrier wagons (various types).
RBX:	Dual-braked Barrier wagons (various types).
RFQ:	Dual-braked Adaptor & Match wagons (various types).

RRA: Air-braked Runner wagons (various air-braked designs).
RRO: Non-fitted Runner wagons (various types).
RRV: Vacuum-braked Runner wagons (various types).
RTV: Vacuum-braked Diesel Brake Tenders).
SAA: Air-braked 400046 – 400249 (many recoded).
SAB: Dual-braked 400000 – 400045 (many recoded).
SBA: Air-braked 400250 – 400299 (many recoded).
SOV: Vacuum-braked 12T Pipe wagons (B740000 – B741949).
SPA: Air-braked 460000 – 461101 (many recoded).
SPO: Non-fitted 22T Plate wagons (B930000 – B931974, with gaps).
SPV: Vacuum-braked 22T Plate wagons (B930000 – B935624, with gaps).
STV: Vacuum-braked 22T Tube wagons (B73000-999, B731590-3219, B733240-459).
UCV: Vacuum-braked 13T China Clay wagons (B743000 – B743874).
ULV: Converted STV wagons for ale pallets.
USV: Vacuum-braked 13T Sand wagons (B746000 – B746849).
UUV: Vacuum-braked TIMBER P wagons.
UYV: Vacuum-braked 25T Anhydrite wagons (B747000 – B747149).
UZP: Converted HTP wagons for aluminous oxide.
UZV: Converted HKV wagons for clinker.
VAA: Air-braked 200550 – 200649.
VAB: Air-braked 200000 – 200218.
VBA: Air-braked 200220 – 200324.
VBB: Air-braked 200000 – 200324.
VCA: Air-braked 200325 – 200549.
VDA: Air-braked 200650 – 201099, 210100 – 210399.
VEA: Air-braked 230000 – 230549.
VEV: Vacuum-braked 12T Vanwide vans (if fitted with roller bearings).
VIX: Dual-braked Ferry vans.
VQB: Dual-braked 22T Pallet Vans.
VQW: Dual-braked 22T Pallet Vans.
VVV: Vacuum-braked 12T Ventilated Vans.
VWV: Vacuum-braked 12T Vanwide vans (B782873-4766, B784773-872).
XCO: Non-fitted Concrete Beam wagons (various types).
XKB: Dual-braked Nuclear Flask wagons.
XLO: Non-fitted Lowmac wagons (various types).
XLP: Vacuum-piped Lowmac wagons (various types).
XLV: Vacuum-braked Lowmac wagons (various types).
XLW: Dual-braked Lowmac wagons (various types).
XRP: Vacuum-piped Rectank wagons.
XUV: Vacuum-braked TRESTLE AA wagons (B903649 – B903664).
XVA: Air-braked 990000 – 990049.
XWP: Vacuum-piped Weltrol wagons.
XYV: Vacuum-braked BOILER EB wagon (B902805 – B902808).

In 1982, the J range of codes was merged with the B range and some codes were used for a second time; this is indicated. The same applied to the K range of codes, which were merged with the S range.

For the sake of clarity, certain codes that did not appear until after the period covered by this volume have been included here.

Listing here depends on photographic confirmation; my apologies if I've missed any, as I obviously never saw the use myself. On all printed documents, the code would have been used, even if it did not appear on the wagon. The number was the important factor.

Wagon Liveries and Lettering

The lettering style and use of code names, which commenced circa 1964, continued unchanged. The introduction of the TOPS code caused a bit of duplication, HOP21HTV and COIL Krv being two oddities noted, but this soon settled down to the codes listed on the previous pages.

Livery Changes

Traditional Fleet

The unfitted rebuilds in the 16T Mineral and 21T Mineral wagon fleets and the JXO Bogie Coil wagons were painted in rail grey livery. The post-1977 rebuilds numbered in the B290000 and B345000 ranges were painted in freight brown, presumably because, with TOPS wagon data, unfitted wagons no longer needed to be identified visually. All other "new" traditional types and any repaints were also freight brown livery.

Air-braked Fleet

The earliest examples, excluding the HAA fleet, were the OAA wagons. These appeared with the code OPEN AB and were painted freight brown. These were followed by the early vans (coded VAN AB and VAN CD) and the four-wheeled steel wagons (coded STEEL AB); both were in freight brown. The vans carried the BR double arrow symbol in white.

In the early 1970s, the AIR BRAKED NETWORK was set up; this was identified by a yellow disc transfer with ABN in black. My own photographs record this from 1975 but it was probably earlier than this.

By 1977, a new livery had been developed. Certain types, such as the OBA, SPA prototypes, VDA and early VEA, were painted maroon with the double arrow symbol and Railfreight name in a lined box panel. Other types, such as the BCA, BDA and HBA, were painted freight brown with similar symbols.

By the end of the review period, a new livery of flame red for later BBA, later BDA OCA and SPA wagons, or rail grey/flame red for ODA and later VEA, had been introduced; the double arrow and Railfreight symbols were retained.

Some attempt was made to repaint existing vehicles in the current livery and certain vans, for instance, appeared in freight brown, maroon and rail grey/flame red. Some even got repainted into the next livery change (to sectors, which will be covered in detail in the next volume). So, at any one time, a variety of livery patterns would be seen.

B290309 taken at Stoke-on-Trent in August 1980. The introduction of TOPS eliminated the need to keep a special colour for unfitted stock and this MDO is in freight brown, unlike the one on the left, which was built just at the introduction of TOPS. (Author's Ref No W8096/DL)

E87857 taken at Ellesmere Port, Wirral in February 1982. Full repaints for vehicles such as this former Insulated Fish van, transferred to become a barrier, were rare and this example retains the old white livery in a very dirty condition. (Author's Ref No W10512/DL)

TDB893448 taken at Stoke-on-Trent in November 1975. In the early TOPS period non-revenue earning vehicles used by the operating department were prefixed TD and were considered departmental stock, as this former cattle wagon. (Author's Ref No W6263/DL)

400114 taken at Doncaster, South Yorkshire in August 1980. Air-braked wagons with little bodywork did not usually receive repaints when the livery was changed for that particular fleet. This STEEL AB has merely had the code changed and still retains a very weathered freight brown livery. (Author's Ref No W8786/DL)

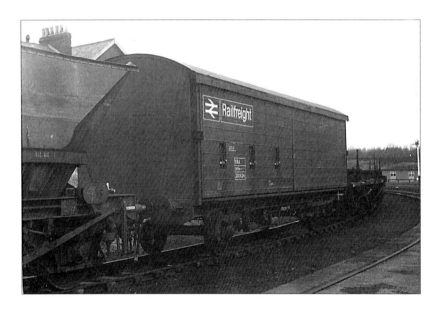

200624 taken at Chester Wagon Works in February 1979. Vans were the usual standard-bearers of the new image. This van was built just before the introduction of the Railfreight brand and was in freight brown livery. Here it is seen repainted in maroon with the full set of symbols. (Author's Ref No W6527/DL)

200760 taken at Briton Ferry, South Wales in April 1977. The maroon livery, when new as seen on these VDA vans, was quite impressive but it tended to fade very quickly to an almost freight brown shade. The next livery was far more colourful and will be covered in the next volume. (Author's Ref No W5597/DL)

Wagon Descriptions

Rebuilt 16T Mineral Wagons (Unfitted)

The problem of body rot for coal-carrying wagons was well-known by the 1960s and it had long been policy to cut out and replace lower side panels. By the late 1960s, this had been changed and complete new bodywork was placed on existing chassis. The 16T mineral wagon fleet was the first to be dealt with and the first examples were appearing by 1969.

Far too many were done for me to be able to keep a record. The new bodywork retained the end door but dropped the flap side doors and this is a tell-tale indicator of a rebuilt vehicle. Not so obvious is the fact that the end door did not always match up with the chassis. On un-rebuilt vehicles viewed from the side, the end door was always to the left on the side with brakeshoes and rigging. This was not always the case with the rebuilds.

Only the welded vehicles of diagram 1/108 seem to have been included in the programme. The riveted wagons built to diagram 1/109 appear to have been withdrawn when found with severe body rot. Consequently, I have no photographs of any of the 1/109 wagons with the MCO code and few lasted beyond the mid-1970s.

The rebodying of diagram 1/108 wagons, as far as unfitted vehicles were concerned, commenced circa 1969 and ceased circa 1976. By 1981, many had been condemned and were broken up. A handful passed to the civil engineers fleet as spoil wagons; these were given the ZHO code and will be covered in another volume.

B242227 taken at Hafodrynys Colliery, South Wales in January 1976. Although not a recent rebody, the rail grey livery of this vehicle stands out when compared with the vehicles either side, which have side panel inserts. None of these has received a painted TOPS code but the vacuum-braked wagon in the foreground is coded MCV. It also has a metric tare weight, which came in about this time. Tare weight: 7-14. (Author's Ref No W6011/DL)

B90231 taken at Battersea in May 1976. This example has been rebodied some time and has received the new data panel with MCO code, 16.5T rating and metric tare; note the different size of the code on the vehicle to the right. All three are loaded with scrap metal, a more usual load than coal in some areas at this time. (Author's Ref No W6568/DL)

B227719 taken at Middlesbrough in October 1975. This wagon is a recent rebody, possibly at the nearby wagon works at Shildon. Curiously, it retains the old COAL 16 code and 16T rating but has a metric tare. Note the tail lamp hanging on the coupling. This is on a goods line in a heavily industrialised area and brake vans appear to have been dispensed with. (Author's Ref No W5977/DL)

B166760 taken at Okehampton, Devon in July 1981. This condemned wagon is one that has been fitted with the new body the wrong way round, as it were, with door to the right on the brakegear side. Both the MCO code and the metric tare are present but the rating is the old Imperial 16T, indicating very little standardisation in lettering at this time. (Author's Ref No W9549/DL)

Rebuilt 16T Mineral Wagons (Vacuum-braked, 9ft 0in wheelbase)

The vacuum-braked 16T minerals were dealt with in a similar manner to the unfitted examples.
However, as well as the welded vehicles of diagram 1/108, a handful of the riveted wagons built to diagram 1/109 appear to have been given new bodies. The 1966 late vacuum-fitted vehicles were also included in the programme.

The rebodying started later and continued for longer, as the vacuum-braked vehicles were generally newer than the unfitted stock, commencing circa 1974 and ceasing circa 1979.

These lasted in service well into the late 1980s in revenue-earning traffic. Many then passed to the civil engineers fleet as spoil wagons; these were given the ZHV code and will be covered in another volume.

B550289 taken at Rochester, Kent in June 1974. This is an early rebodied wagon and has both pre-TOPS code and rating and Imperial tare. It is "wrong-way-round" in respect to the end door. Tare weight: 8-2. (Author's Ref No W4618/DL)

B558201 taken at Nunhead, South East London in April 1977. By contrast, this later rebody has full TOPS code and metric rating and tare weight. The vehicle to the right has only the overpainted metric tare. Once again, the end door is "wrong-way round". (Author's Ref No W6768/DL)

B261574 taken at Sheerness, Kent in July 1980. This is a former diagram 1/109 riveted wagon. Obviously, the vacuum-brakegear took priority over bodywork although I have only recorded three such wagons. Judging by the data panel, it was always coded MCV, with metric rate and tare weight. (Author's Ref No W8398/DL)

B572477 taken at Burry Port, South Wales in August 1981. Seen with an impressive load, this is one of the 1966 vacuum-braked vehicles and the data panel, with MCV code and metric rate and tare weight are original. The end door is "wrong-way-round". (Author's Ref No W9583/DL)

B590180 taken at Brixton, South West London in July 1978. With yet another "wrong-way-round" body, this example is loaded with metal swarf and filings. Such a load did not require flap doors and nor did local coal merchants, as these had been eliminated. (Author's Ref No W6913/DL)

Rebuilt 16T Mineral Wagons (Vacuum-braked, 10ft 0in wheelbase)

A curious batch of rebodied vehicles had 10ft 0in wheelbase. These, in fact, were not originally 16T Minerals but were Palbrick wagons. In view of the relatively small number built and the fact that British Rail had established just how many MCV wagons it had in the fleet when the TOPS computer began operating, I believe that this was a programme authorised to alleviate the problems caused by workshop closures, the Lancashire-located Horwich works in this case. New numbers in the 16T Mineral series were issued and these were as follows:

B596000 to B596393   16.5T MCV MINERAL   8/1975 to 4/1978   3863   BR (Horwich)

No single diagram could be issued because, although the bodywork was the same, the chassis details were not, although all had 10ft 0in wheelbase. Numbers, and chassis details, were as follows:

MCV (8-shoe Brakegear, Oil axleboxes and 1ft 6in OLEO Spindle buffers):
B596069, B596113/52/61.

MXV (4-shoe Brakegear, Oil axleboxes and 1ft 6in Spindle buffers):
B596000-8/10/2-6/8/9/20-34/6/8-40/2-52/4-68/70-88/90-9, B596100-12/4/49/53-5/7-60/2-75/7-97/9, B596200/1/3-18/20-34/6-41/3/4/6-56/8-70/2-99, B596300/1/3-43/5-54/5/7-75/8-88/91-3.

MCV (8-shoe Brakegear, Roller Bearings and 1ft 8½in OLEO Hydraulic buffers):
B596009/11/7/25/35/7/53, B596202/35/42/5/71, B596302/56/76/7/89/90.

The majority of these wagons, together with those vacuum-braked numbered between B560200 and B583299, whether rebodied or not, had 4-shoe brakegear. Those with 8-shoe brakegear caused a problem at Goole, a port on the East Coast where coal was exported and where the wagons were lifted by crane suspended on cradles and tipped into the holds of vessels, the load of coal passing out from the end door. The code MXV was retrospectively given to the 4-shoe brakegear vehicles, circa 1982, to prevent those coded MCV being loaded to Goole.

B596161 taken at Hoo Junction, Rochester in September 1981. This rebody was based on B459251 and, having LMS-pattern 8-shoe vacuum brakegear, also remained an MCV. Lettering, in this case, was full TOPS code with metric rate and tare weight. (Author's Ref No W9245/DL)

B596192 taken at Foxton, Cambridgeshire in April 1979. Although built well after the introduction of TOPS codes, certain of these vehicles were coded COAL 16 VB and Imperial 16T rate. In this case it also seems to have an overpainted metric tare weight. The vehicle of origin was B462089. (Author's Ref No: W7745/DL)

B596212 taken at Silvertown, East London in August 1980. This example has a very crude MCV code overpainting the original lettering but the rate and metric tare weight look original. The source vehicle in this case was B462149. (Author's Ref No 8465/DL)

B596315 taken at Worksop, Nottinghamshire in February 1983. This would have been one of the 1978-built vehicles and would have been an MCV originally; it now has the MXV code. No body rot seems to have afflicted these wagons; perhaps they were constantly on the move and never stored loaded. (Author's Ref No W12529/DL)

Rebuilt 21T Mineral Wagons (Unfitted, 1975–76 rebuilds)

This group of vehicles was probably built to serve the Welsh export coal from Swansea, which was normally carried in 21T capacity mineral wagons. Some of these became unavailable through age, notably the former private owner vehicles which could still be seen well into the early 1970s (a few withdrawn examples survived into 1976). The bodywork resembled the diagram 1/107 welded 21T Mineral of 1951/52 in all details and second-hand chassis were used. Source vehicles were mixed and, although all these vehicles were unfitted, chassis and brakegear details varied greatly. The number series was as follows:

B315000 to B317599   21T MINERAL NF   3/1975 to 7/1976   None   Various works   COAL 21 (MDO)

LNE 21T Coal Hopper pattern brakegear
B315122, B315261, B315326/63, B315426, B316029, B316140, B316507/9/10/62,
B316605 /10/27/8 /50/8/68//72/4/82/90-2, B316711/5/8/20/6-9/36-8/41-5/7/8/50/65/6/8/9/80/1/4/92/3,
B316804/7/10/1/3/20/35/40-2/4/6/7/50/5-9/63/6/71/8/80-3/90/3/4/8,
B316900/4/13-5/9/24/5/31-3/44/6-9/53-5/7/69/71/6/8/80/6/90-6, B317013/4/7/21/47/9/61/3/81/6/9/99,
B317102/28/32/7/42/ 5/6/8/72/5-7, B317211, B317301/7/8/16/38/9.

BR 21T Morton brakegear with spindle buffers
B315001-5/7-18/21-33/7/8/40-76/9-94/7-9, B315102-12/4-9/21-30/2/4-40/2-5/7/9/50-6/8-65/7-9/71/3-5/7-87/9-99, B315200-12/4-23/5-30/2-45/7-53/5-61/3/4/6-71/3-85/7-97/9, B315300-3/5-7/9-20/2-5/8-62/4-70/2-83/6-99,
B315400-5/7-9/11-23/5/7-41/3-8/50-64/6-95/7/8, B315500-25/7-63/5-9/71-4/6/8-84/6-93/6-9,
B315600-6/8-10/2/3/6-20/3/4/6-8/30/3-8/40-4/6-50/2/3-8/60/1/3-5-85/7-99,
B315700-2/4-23/5-30/2-5/7-40/2-50/3-7/9/61-8/70-80/2/6-99,
B315800/2-20/2-5/7-34/7-9/41-56/8-67/9-76/8-86/9-99, B315900-23/5-8/31-5/7-44/6-52/4-70/4/5/7-99,
B316000-3/5-13/5/6/8-28/30-54/7-73/5-80/2-6/8-92/4-9,
B316100/2/4-8/10-9/21/2/4-8/30/2-4/6-8/41-6/8-51/3-7/9-65/8-70/3-7/9-94/6-9,
B316200-11/3-8/20-45/7-56/8/60-83/5-99, B316300-27/30-2/4/5/7-40/3-50/2-5/7-70/2-4/6-95/8/9,
B316400-3/5-20/2-5/7/30-7/40/1/3-55/7-62/4/6/7/9-72/4-7/9/81-7/90-7/9,
B316500-6/8/12/3/7-9/21-7/9/30/2-4/6/8/9/41-7/9/50/3-61/3-72/4-7/80-91/5-9,
B316600-4/6-9/11-4/6/20-3/5/6/9/30/2/4-9/41/2/4/6/9/53-5/7/60-4/6/7/9-71/3/5/6/81/4-9/93-6/8/9,
B316700-8/13/4/7/9/21-5/30-3/5/9/40/6/9/51-61/3/4/7/70-9/83/5/6/8-91/4/6/8/9,
B316800-3/5/6/8/9/12-9/21/2/4-34/6-9/43/5/8/51-3/60-2/4/5/7/70-2-7/9/84-9/91/6/7/9,
B316901/3/5-8/10-2/6-8/20-3/6-8/30/4-8/40-3/5/52/6/8-66/8/70/2-5/7/9/81/2/4/5/8/9/97-9,
B317000-3/5/6/8-12/5/6/8/20/2-9/31/3-5/8/9/41-3/5/6/8/50-6/8-60/2/5/7-72/4-7/80/3-5/7/8/90-8,
B317100/1/3/6-10/2-7/9/20/2-7/9/31/3-6/8-41/3/4/9/51/4-71/3/4/8-90/2-5/7-9,
B317200-2/4-8/12-4/9/21/3-7/9/31-47/50-3/5-8/60-3/5-8/70/2-7/80/2/6-90/2/6-9,
B317300/2-5/9/11/2/4/5/7-28/30-4/6/7/40-6/8/9/51/4-73/6-94/7/8,
B317400-12/5-7/9/21-4/6/7/9-41/3/5-70/2/3/5/7-85/7-92/4-9, B317500.

BR 21T Morton brakegear with self contained buffers
B315000/6/19/20/34/5/6/9/77/8/95, B315100/1/13/31/3/41/6/8/57/66/70/2/88,
B315213/24/31/46/54/65/72/86/98, B315304/8/21/44/71/84, B315406/10/24/42/9/65/96, B315526/64/70/5/7/85,
B315607/11/4/5/21/2/5/9/31/2/9/45/51/9/62/4/86, B315703/24/36/41/58/60/9/81/3-5,
B315801/21/6/35/6/40/57/68/77/87/8, B315924/9/30/6/45/53/71-3/6, B316004/55/6/74/81/7/90/3,
B316101/3/9/23/9/31/5/9/47/52/8/66/7/71/2/8/95, B316212/9/46/57/9/84, B316328/9/33/6/41/2/51/6/71/5/96/7,
B316404/21/6/8/9/38/9/42/56/63/5/8/73/8/80/8/9/98, B316511/4-6/20/8/31/5/7/40/8/51/2/73/8/9/93/4,
B316615/7/8/24/31/3/48/51/2/6/9/65/77-80/3/97, B316709/12/6/34/62/87/97, B316849/54/68/9/92/5,
B316902/9/29/39/50/1/67/83/7, B317004/7/19/30/2/6/7/40/4/57/64/6/8/9/82, B317104/5/11/8/21/47/50/2/96,
B317203/9/10/3/20/2/8/30/49/54/69/71/8/81/3-5/91/3/4, B317313/29/35/47/50/2/74/5/95/6/9,
B317413/4/8/20/5/8/42/71/4/6/86/93

BR 21T Morton brakegear with OLEO hydraulic buffers and roller bearings
B315096, B315120/76, B315499, B315731/51, B316014/7, B316120, B316710, B317248/95, B317310.

BR 24.5T Hopper (LNE-pattern eight-shoe brakegear with spindle buffers)
B315594/5, B316619/40/3/5/7, B316782, B316823, B317191, B317259.

BR 24.5T Hopper (BR-pattern four-shoe brakegear with roller bearings and self-contained buffers)
B316795, B317073, B317191, B317264.

Roller bearings were fitted to many vehicles, not just the listed batches. These had them from new, whilst odd vehicles had them retro-fitted. These wagons lasted into the mid-1980s.

B315039 taken in Harecastle, Staffordshire in August 1980. This example had been in service for roughly five years and it shows that little effort had been wasted on paint. The number panel has TOPS code MDO and metric tare. (Author's Ref No W8061/DL)

B316782 taken at Stoke-on-Trent, Staffordshire in November 1975. The bulk of the fleet was built using standard Morton 21T unfitted brakegear but some more unusual chassis were also used. This example is based on an early 24½T chassis from B333019 and has received roller bearings a lot earlier. (Author's Ref No W5021/DL)

DB316978 taken at Tees Yard, Middlesbrough in May 1981. This wagon has unusually been transferred to the civil engineers department at a time when most of the fleet was still in revenue-earning traffic. The TOPS code actually relates to 16T Minerals wagons, so this could be an erroneous transfer. (Author's Ref No W9666/DL)

Rebuilt 21T Mineral Wagons (1977–78 rebuilds)

The second group of vehicles were, quite frankly, rather unnecessary and were probably ordered to alleviate problems over the closure of Ashford and Shildon works. The bodywork was a new design with no end door and a single side door at the left-hand end (thus being diagonal when viewed from above). The chassis used were recovered from 21T Mineral wagons, 24½T Mineral wagons and 24½T Coal Hopper wagons. There was a further complication as regards numbering. If the original springs were retained, so was the original number; if new five-leafed springs were fitted, a new metric rate of 25.0tonnes was applied and new numbers given. The number series was as follows:

B290000 to B290485   25Tonnes MDO (Min)   6/1977 to 5/1978   3920 BR (Ashford)   BR (Shildon)

Of these, B290200, B290210 and B290214 were vacuum-braked and were coded MDV. Another five (B310782, B310839, B311411, B312313 and B312558) retained the original springs and numbers.

As far as the unfitted stock, these can be separated by brakegear as follows:

21T Morton unfitted brakegear with spindle buffers
B200002/6/24/30/1/8/45/50/6/60/8/71/9/86/9/91/4, B200101/6/10/1/5/22/37/69/78/87/92/6, B200205/7/9
/19/26/30/1/58/60/1/9/83/7/93/9, B200300/15/22/5/32/6/8/56/67/76/81, B200409/12/6/29/31/50/1/60/5/6
/82/7/91, B200500/3/17/27/8/31/45/51/68/81/91, B200601/13/5/8-20/33/4/44/9/51/5/86/92, B200701/38
/54/6/63/8/83, B200823/37/64/5/75/7/9/81/7, B200906/15/36/8/40/51/61/7/73, B201014/9/24/32/9/45/52
/6/64/6/80, B201113/6/7/21/40/1/52/7/73/6/84/90/2/6/7, B201200/3-5/14/8/35/9/44/72/81/6/97, B201318
/27/30/5/44/64/81, B201404/21/38/44/7/9/58/73/9/81/95, B201513/4/9/26/9/31/63/88/93/6, B201602/10
/29/41/8/66/71, B201703/4/28, B201815, B201946/52/90, B202003/4/10/9/23/30/8/46/51/4/5/7/61/4/8/78
/82/7/91/2/5-9, B202104/9/28/43/8/54/5/61/2/9/72/3/9/81/4/8/90/6/7/9, B202201/3/8/11/3/8/22/5/8/30/3/4
/45/59/64/8/76/84/8/93, B202309/18/9/47/54/5/63/7/71/81/4/94/6, B202400/5/6/9/14/20/5/33-5/48/51/6/60
/2/6/7/81/2; B290000/3-6/8/9/14/6/9/28/39/42/3/56, B290105/8/20-3/8/30/1/9/45/53/60/9/72/5-7/80/1/7/8
/95-7, B290223-9/32/5-7/9/44/59/69/70/4/82-4/6/8/9/98/9, B290300/4-7/12/5/6/9/22/4/7-9/34-6/9-41/5/7-
52/4/8/60-3/5/6/9/71/3/84/5/7/91/3/4/8, B290400/7/8/13/4/9/20/2/3/7/9/41/2/5-8/50/2-4/6/9/61-4/73/5-7/
83/4.

B200877 taken at Stoke-on-Trent, Staffordshire in August 1980. Most of the 21T Mineral conversions had received roller bearings before being rebodied but reference to photographs shows some retained oil axleboxes. The livery was always freight brown and lettering appropriate to the metric TOPS period. (Author's Ref No W8069/DL)

17

B290014 taken at Peak Forest, Derbyshire in February 1980. This wagon has been renumbered, as it has been fitted with five-leaf springs; the original number was B200387. At this stage, they were rated 25T but this was found excessive and all were downrated to 21.5T in time. (Author's Ref No W8088/ DL)

24.5T Morton unfitted brakegear with oil axleboxes and spindle buffers
B280002/6/9/17/8/24/9/31/2/8/9/45/7/50/7/70/87/91/3, B280105/17/20-2/5/8/40/54/69/76/83/8/98/9, B280202/4/7/13/8/64/99, B280307/10/47/52/66/79/87, B280405/18/33/5/47/50/63/4/70-2/87/97, B280530/40/1/53-5/9, B280618/39/51/3/9/62/4/7/71/2/4/5/9/83/4/7-90/5/7-9, B280701/3/14-6/20/34/42 /50/8/71/2/4/6/80/3/91/3/6/8, B280804/6/8/9/12/4/5/8/20/5/30/5/9/41-3/6/7/9/53/4/6/60/4/9/77/8/82/4/5/8 /91/6/9, B280903/11-4/7/20/3/4/7/31/2/6/8/40-2/54/7/60/2/73/7/8/85/97, B281003/8/9/15/6/23/5/9/31/3/4 /43/5/8/9/51/3-5/8/61-6/71/6/8-80/2/5-9/91/2, B281100/4/5/10/1/3-6/8/9/21/6/8/34/7-9/42/5/6/9/59/60/4/9 /72/7/82/6/93, B281202/8/9/13/23-5/8/9/33/4/40/7/8/53/62/74/83/5/6/92/5, B281308/9/16/9/20/4/38-40/4 /6/56/7/9/63/70/6/80/7/91, B281402/6/15/21/7/33/41/3/5/6/52/6/61/2/3/73/7/8/80/3/90/1/3/6, B281526/32/4 /47/50/2/79/87-9/94/5/7, B281602/10/1/3-6/21/5/31/4/47/50/1/8/60/6/72/8/90/1/5, B281702/4/8/13/4/27/8 /39/44/54/5/61/5/6/8-71/3/82/5/9/93/5, B281813/5/21-3/5/32/47-9/55/60/2/8-70/4/85/7-92/4/5, B281903/6 /8/11/2/4-6/8/20/1/7/30-3/6-8/40/4-6/8/50/1/4/71/2/6/80/3/4/7/8/90-2/8, B282002/4/11/2/20/2/5/33/5-7/9-43 /7/8/50-3/5/6/61/3/4/70/1/4/7/84/6/91/5/6/9, B282106/7/10/4/9/22/3/5/6/8/9/34/8/9/45/9, B290001/7/11-3/5 /7/8/20/1/3/5/7/9/30/2-8/41/4/51/5/8/61/70-2/5/7/8/80/2/4-7/9/90/2/5, B290103/6/9-13/5/8/9/25/6/9/32/4/5 /7/40/2/3/7/8/50/4/5/7-9/61-3/5/7/70/1/8/82/4-6/94, B290220/1/30/4/42/5/7/9/51-5/60/1/4-7/71-3/5/7/9/85/7 /90-3/5, B290308/9/11/3/8/20/1/3/5/30-2/8/43/6/53/6/7/64/8/70/2/4-83/6/8-90/5/7/9, B290401/11/2/5-8/4-6 /8/30-4/6/8-40/9/51/5/7/8/60/6-70/4/8-82/5.

24.5T Morton unfitted brakegear with roller bearings and self-contained buffers
B282166/73/89, B282214/26/9/38/41/58/62/3/6/70-2/4/8/9, B282305/8/12/5/20/9/34/6/45/59/66/7/82/5/92-4, B282412/5/6/9/26/7/9/36/43/6/53/9/64/7/77/9/83/5/8/92/4/6, B282513/40/2/4/6/8/9/66/7, B282609/12 /33/9/42/6-8/51-3/6/66/71/3/7/85-7/93, B282702/7/9/11/9/22, B290002/10/26/54/60/74/91, B290101/14 /73/99, B290263/76/97, B290310/7/33/7/44/55/92, B290402/4-6/9/21/65.

24.5T Morton unfitted brakegear with roller bearings and OLEO hydraulic buffers
B282770/3/4/80/3/94/7/8, B282802/8/17-9/24/36/40/4/7/51/5/64/98/9, B282906/12/4/7/9/24/7/30/4/9/41-3 /5/9/55/7/63/82/3/7/92, B283063/9/70, B283107/10/78/95, B283206/23/37/8/44/7/9/55/8/66/8/76/84/7/94, B283307/8/12/21/34/6/8/70, B290024/31/40/52/3/73, B290104/16/7/24/66/8/79, B290241/3, B290314/42 /59/67/96, B290403/10/35/7.

24.5T Hopper (LNE-pattern eight-shoe brakegear with spindle buffers)
B290146.

24.5T Hopper (BR-pattern four-shoe brakegear with roller bearings and self-contained buffers)
B290022/45-50/59/62-9/76/9/81/3/8/93/4/6-9, B290102/7/27/33/6/8/41/4/9/51/2/6/64/74/83/9-93/8, B290222/31/3/8/40/6/8/50/6-8/62/8/78/80/1/96, B290302/3/26.

B282436 taken at Burry Port, South Wales in March 1983. This example has the self-contained buffers and roller-bearings of the second variation of diagram 1/115. As there was only one side door per side, one set of door bangers was omitted. (Author's Ref No W12713/ DL)

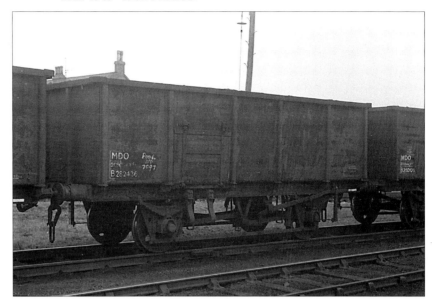

B290392 taken at Toton Yard in February 1983. The original number of this wagon was B282462. Given five-leaf springs, it was renumbered and rated at 25Tonnes. This view illustrates this particular example after it has been derated and the number box has been crudely amended. (Author's Ref No W12661/ DL)

B290144 taken at Swansea, South Wales in March 1983. A similar history to that of B290392 above is illustrated here. The original chassis, however, came from the 24½T Coal Hopper B335480. Not having door bangers originally, those wagons with this chassis had a single door banger. (Author's Ref No W12765/DL)

Rebuilt 21T Coal Hopper Wagons (1971-78 rebuilds)

This group of rebuilds covered a comparable period to that of the 16T Mineral wagons. The identification feature here was the side, which had two vertical stanchions only, rather than five. There were, however, some variations.

The early unfitted rebuilds were painted rail grey and were coded HOP 21, then HOP21HTO and finally just HTO. If vacuum-braked, the livery was freight brown with HOP 21 VB, HOP21HTV and finally HTV codes.

The second group of vehicles were had a similar origin to the single-door MDO fleet but only Shildon works was involved this time. The bodywork was as the previous batches but some had inverted stanchions, which gave a different appearance to the sides. If original springs were retained, so was the original number; if new five-leafed springs were fitted, a new metric rate of 25.0tonnes was applied and new numbers given. Both unfitted and vacuum-braked batches were involved and the number series were as follows:

B340000 to B340924	25Tonnes HTV Hopper	3/1977 to 4/1978	3916 BR (Shildon)	Vac-braked
B345000 to B346468	25Tonnes HTO Hopper	4/1977 to 6/1978	3919 BR (Shildon)	Unfitted

(Note: B340914 to B340922 and B346359 to B346410/2/5 to 59 were not built.)

Only former 21T Coal hopper chassis were used and these have been separated by brakegear. No record was ever kept for those with inverted U-channel stanchions (known as "Hucks Bolt" bodies).

Unfitted with LNE pattern single-side brakegear
B345004/5/7/9-11/3-20/4/7-9/31-46/9/50/2-65/7-71/3-5/8-84/6-99, B345100/2-7/10-4/6/7/9/21/2/4-8/30-5/7-9/42-7/9-57/9-80/2-6/-99, B345200-15/7-27/9-38/40-3/5-53/5-7/9-65/7-97/9, B345300-13/6-20/2-54/6/7/60-78/81-93/5/6/8/9, B345400-7/9-15/7-24/6-41/3-5/7-57/9-61/3/6-8/70/1/4/5/7-91/3-9, B345500-15/7-22/4-47/9-59/62-88/90-9, B345600-3/5-12/5/6/8-40/2/4-9/52-82/6/7/9/92-6/8/9, B345700-16/8/9/21/3/6—51/3-70/2/4-70/2/4-81/4-99, 345800-4/6/8-22/4-30/2-40/2-54/7-70/2-9/82/3/5/6/8-99, B345900-27/9-50/2/4-67/9/99, B346000-9/11-20/2-9/32-50/2-61/3-99, B346100-4/6-15/7-23/5-36/8-42/4-51/3-77/9-86/8-99, B346200-12/4-38/40-53/5-88/90-9, B346301-20/2-58, B346411/3/4/60-8; B410000/1/3/4/7/11/2/6/8/212/4/6/8/9/31/2/4-6/8/9/42/3/50/5/6/63/4/7/72/4/81/3/4/-7-9/92, B410104/5/10/2/4/7/20/6/32/42/9/52/7/9/69/78/80/2/7/8/93/4, B410201/8-10/2/4/6/29/33/4/6/8/48/50/60/2/8/76/80/1/6/96, B410300/9/22/3/9/33/6/7/9/40/2/5-7/55/71/2/4/8/85/9/94, B410400/1/9/11/4/9/20/5/9/32/40/5/50/4/6/61/70/1/5/6/84/6/7/9/95-7/9, B410502/6/7/11/8/9/23/8/47/9/53/9/66/78/81/5/91/5, B410605/8/17/20/2/30/2/5/8/40/51/62/4/9/70/5/9-81/6/7/9/91/3, B410704/23/30/7-9/49/51/8/66/86/7/97/8, B410800/14/6/20/3/7/34/7/43/64/6/9/70/83/6/91, B410906/11/3/31/6-9/42/3/9/58/62/8/75/7/9/82/6/95, B411005/7/8/19/23/7/31/2/42-4/7/50/1/4/5/8/64/81/4/6/7/9/95/6, B411100/1/3/11-4/8/20-2/4/30/1/3/6/8-41/6/7/50/2/5/7/8/61/4/8/80/3/5/97, B411201-4/6-8/10/1/4-6/9/21/5/6/30/7-40/4-8/50-3/5/6/8/60/2/5-9/72/3/7/80-5/8/9/91/4/5/7-9, B411300/1/5/7/11-3/6/7/9/21-3/6-8/30/2/4/5/8/41/3/5/6/51/2/7-9/62/5/6/8/77-9/81/3/5/7-92/5-7, B411403/4/6/10/3-6/9/21/3/4/6/32-6/41/3/5/7/50-5/7/60-4/8-70/4-6/9-83/5/7/8/90/2/4/6, B411500/2-7/9-12/7-20/2/3/5/7/8/33/5/6/8/9/41/3/6-/51/2/4-7/62/3/6/70/3-5/80/2/6/7/9/90/3/4, B411603/7/10/3/5-7/25/30/2/40/3/6/50/9/63/7/78/81/9/97, B411708/13/9/20/4/5/8/33/4/7/42/4/5/50/1/9/60/5/7/8/83/4/6/8-90/3, B411801/6/11/3-6/20/1/4/6/31-3/6/9/40/4/7/50/2/3/60/4/9/72/4/6/7/83/5/8/90/3/4/8, B411900-3/5-8/10/3/21/2/4/6/7/30-2/40-2/4/50-3/5/7/9/61/2/4/5/7/72/5-7/82/4/7/8/91/3/7-9, B412001/4/7/10-3/5-7/21/4/6-9/36/9/41/4/7-9/51/3/4/73/80/2/4/8-90, B412104/10/1/3/25/9/58/69/70/2/8/88/93/5/7-9, B412201/6/16/28/30/2/5-7/9/48/9/60/75/91/2/5/7, B412300/18/20/5/9/35/9/52/5/7/68/74/82/5-8/92/3/6, B412400-2/5/12/6/8/20/1/4/8/30/2/6/7/40/4/55/60/5/6/9/73/5/81, B412508/9/11/2/8/22/7/9/32/4/59/60/3/8/82/8/99, B412600/7/9/20/2/8/30/2/6/7/54/6/7/60-2/4/71/81/6/90/5/6/8, B412700/2/6/16/9/20/30/2/52/8/9/62/6/70/5/7/9/81/2/5/7/9/90/5/6/8, B412801-3/6/7/9/15-9/22/3/6/9/36-8/44/5/7/9/53/4/66-8/72/6/9/81/7/9-91/4/8, B412902/10/2/5/6/21/4/6/8/30/3-5/41/5/6/52/60/6/9-71/3/95,

B410072 taken at Brierley Hill, Staffordshire in September 1982. This is a relatively early rebody in very patchy rail grey livery with an overpainted number panel with the HTO code. Oil axleboxes have been retained. (Author's Ref No W11848/DL)

B413001/2/4/9/23/5/6/36/40-3/4/6/51/4-6/8/60-2/4/8/72-4/7/84/7/9/93/5/6, B413102/6/8/9/12/5/20-3/5/9/31/5/6/41/3/4/6/8/51/3/5/7/60-2/4/6/73/4/8/80/5/6/8/91-4/6, B413203-5/7/9/13/8/26-9/31/2/4/5/42/3/6/9/51/6-64/9/73/4/6-80/5/6/91/5/7/9, B413302-4/9/10/4/7/8/24-6/8-31/5-7/44/7/8/50/2-4/6-9/63/6/9/80-2/4-8/92-5/8/9, B413401/2/7/10/2/3/22-4/6/8/30/2/47/52/4/60/8/9/71/3/5/81/3/7-91/3-5, B413504-6/9/11/8/23/5/67/8/31/2/4/43/4/6/7/50/2/6/7/63/5/72-4/6/81/90-2/6/8, B413602/4/9/12/5/23/6/9/33/4/6/8-40/2-8/51-3/6/8/67/8/70/2/3/8/9/82/5/7/9/90/3/5/7, B413710/4/7/21/5/6/31/4/45/7/8/53/4/64/6/75-7/83/6/8/92/3/8, B413805/9/10/29/34/41/2/6/63/9/74/7, B413902/8/17/9/20/4/7/9/39/40, B414052/5/7/8/62/3/71/3-5/7-9/81/4-7/9/90/3-6, B414100/2/3/7-10/4/5/21/6/9/36-8/40/5/53/5/7/60/2-70/3/4/6/9/81-3/90/3/8/9, B414216/8/22/7/9/31/46/8-50/4/5/8-63/5-70/3/4/6/83/6-8/91-4/6/8/9, B414304-6/10/1/3/4/20/2-4/7/31-4/9/40/2/50/1/3-6/9-69/71-3/5/6/9-85/8-90/2/6/7, B414401-5/8/11/3/6/9-22/8/30/1/3-6/8/41/2/4/6/9/52-5/7-61/3/5/7/8/70-2/5/6/81/3/4/6-8/90/2-5/9, B414500/1/3-5/7/11/2/4/5/21/2/5/7/30/1/7/40/4/7/9/53/6/9/64/6/73/9/86/9/92/6, B414600/4/6/8-10/3/5/21-8/37/43/4/7/50/1/4/6/60/2-4/8/76/7/9/81/3/4/8/9/91/2/4/5/9, B414711/3/4/7-9/22-9/34/5/43/6-52/5/8/61/2/4/5/9/72/3/7/8/80/5-8/90/9, B414800/2-4/8/12/7/21/3/4/8/9/33/7/43/5/6/8/51/3/62/3/6/7/9-74/85/8/95/7/8, B414903/12/6/8/20/1/5/7/8/30/2/6-8/41/2/6/7/9/55-7/60/2/7/9/70/3/5/7/9/80/2/5/6/8/91/4/5/8, B415002-4/6/8-11/5/8/20/1/7/9/37/40/3/5/8/9/51-4/9/61-3/5/6/8-70/2/4/7-9/83/4/6/8/95/6, B415100-2/4/6/7/9/12/3/7/8/21/3/5-8/32/6-9/47-9,

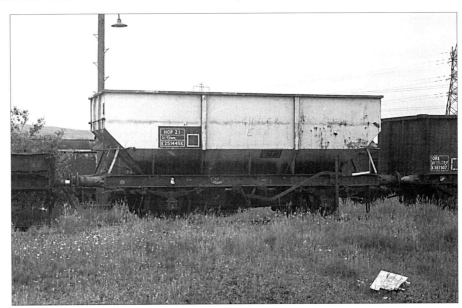

E251445K taken at Swansea Docks, South Wales in April 1975. This early rebody is not listed below. It is based on the wagons built for the Ministry of Supply during WWII which used a continental style chassis with curved brake lever and was very rare. Livery is rail grey with HOP 21 code. (Author's Ref No W4902/DL)

E193261/76, E193312/8/26/41/95, E193408/31/56/60/77, E193513/28/47/51/78, E193602/16/7/66/75, E193712, E205783/90/9, E205827/39/52/93, E205939, E227928/40/64/9, E228055/6/65, E260353/77/81, E260400/1/6/10/2/34/9/47/9/50/2/84/5/95, E260503/4/12/6/20/1/5/34/48/61/75/85/8/99, E260619/23 /32/3/6/48/9/67/89, E260711/23/7/38/81/8, E260806/16/28/31/6/41/3, E269007/12-4/6/21/4/34/7/8/41/9 /53/4/60/72-4/84/9/90/7, E269104/8/17/24/34/44/9/51/8/67/76/91/5, E269204/42/62/86/92, E269311/38 /40/69/75/9, E260407/18/53/5/73/6/84, E269540/51/7/8/65/6/78/83/5/7/90/7, E269614/20/9/30/3/6/40/56 /69/72/80/6/8/9/97/9, E269708/12/9/24/5/8/48/57/72/3/9/84/6, E269852/3/61/79, E269903/23/6/7, E270708/10/21/3-5/7/31/6/41/7/54/8/60/2/9/71/5/8/80/98/9, E270803/5/8/11/2/4/28/32/6/50/3/5/8/62/7 /77/80/1/3/4/7/90/1/3, E270904-6/10/2/4/22/6/7/30/4-6/8/40/8/53/65/81/3/96/9, E271002/3/13/5/22/4/7 /37/9/41/2/7/9/63/7-9/77/82/3/90-2/4, E273623/6/9/32/5/8/40/50/4/5/68/70/2/4/5/80/2/94/5/7/8, E273703 /9/16/8/25/7/31/3/4/7/8/40/4/51/3/4/60/5/6/77/8/88/93, E273800/2/24/6/8/9/31/4/7/42/7/9/53/9-61/6/8/9 /77/85/8/96/9, E273900/7/23/6/7/9-31/6/41-4/7/8/50/3/6/9/60/2/7/8/71/2/5/9/81/5/7/91/2/5, E274005/6 /20/4/9/38/40/1/4/52/3/5/74/6/7/81/4/5/95/7, E274102/11/21/3/6/9/30/2/7/41/4/9/51/4/5/8/67/73/9/84/9 /94/5, E274200/1/9/13/4/26/8-30/5/44/6/7/57/9/67/71/5/81/8/9/91/6/7/9, E274302, E274990/4/9, E275001 /5/10/2/3/24/6/36/8/40/6/50-2/4/6/9/63/5/8/77/8, E289192/3/8, E289200/5/7/8/11/3/21/4/37/8/44/5/55/61 /70/3/8/81/2/4/6/7/9/98, E289318/23/5/9-31/3/6/49/51/3/7/72/3/7/81/7/91/2, E289404/6/10/3/7/8/23/5/36 /8/45/57/60/3/4/71/4/7/87/9709, E289509/17/20/3/4/6/33/5/44/52/61/71/9/92/7, E289601/10/3/5/6/8/21/2 /5/6/8-30/2/4/6/8-40/2/50/6/62/4/7/76/80/6/9/93, E289701-3/10/21/3/7/8/32/9/40/51/4/6/67/9/71/89/93 /5/8, E279800/5/9/13/8/27/9/34/6/8/43/6/7/50/2/5/6/68/71/7/8/82/5/6,

E301861 taken at Hartlepool's Docks in September 1981. This is a post-1977 rebody with inverted U-channel stanchions. This version was officially referred to as fitted with Huck bolts and was produced due to a lack of welders at Shildon. Livery is freight brown. (Author's Ref No W9459/DL)

E301703/4/9/13/6/26/8/30/1/4/6/7/41/3-5/52/60/7/8/70/2/3/5/6/81/5/7/8/90/3/7, E301811/3/8/21/30/1 /40/2/4/5/7/61/4-6/74/80/3/6/7/94/9, E301902/6/16/9/27/45/53/62/4/8/72/81/90, E302003/7/13/5/24/6/7 /31/6/8/42/4/5/52-4/64/70/3/7/92, E302101/5/15/6/9/25/6/36/9/40/3/5/50/8/9/75/9/82/6/9/92/4/5, E302204 /8/10/6/8/24/31/3/9/43/5/6/9/53/7/8/64/9/83/6/9/92/5/6/8, E302310/2/7/20/6/8/37/8/44/7/57/9/64/71/2/4/5 /7/9/81/90/6/8, E302407/10/1/7/9/20/2/5/8/31/4/43/6/58/64/6/73/86/91/3, E302506/9/10/3/8/22/3/6/40/2/4 /6/7/9/56/64/8/9/72/5/8/85/8/93/8/9, E302602/4-6/11/2/4/23/9/31/51/6/7/72/6/80/2/92/5, E302702/11/4/20 /3/5/31/3/40/3/5/55/8/60/2/74-6/84/7/91/4/6-8, E302800/2/5/7-9/12/7/21/30/2/4/51/2/6/9/61/4/71/80/4 /93/8, E302900/6/10/2/24/37/43/7/9/55/7/8/60/2/6/73/5/7/84/5/93, E303002/12/5/24-6/8/9/31/40/1/3/6 /56/64/5/74/80/1/3/6/90/2/4/6, E303100/5/15/6/8/22/6/31/3/8/41-3/8/54/6/9/68/71/2/7/80-2/5/9/90/2/3, E303202/12/5/21/3/30/1/42/4/52/3/9/68/76/7/901, E303301/2/6/14/6/22/3/9/31/3/9/44/8/55/72/5/9-81/94, E303404/17/27/9/38/40/64/72/5/82/4/9/90/4, E303504-6/9/11/42/4/7/9/51/2/60/1/4/6/70/2/5/9/80/91/4 /8/9, E303610/1/7/24/7/9/35/9-41/4/71/3/4/85/91/8, E303704/32/5/8/47/9/52/4/8/60/5/83-6/92/6-8, E303802/6/7/12/31/2/4/40/1/4/9/53/62/77/89/97/9, E303900/3/6/10/8/32/5/6/42/3/7/60/1/4/72/82/91/3, E304002/13/21-4/48/56/74/81/4/5/9/90/3/4, E304100/7/19/21/8/42/4/5/50/5/9/60/5/72/9/83/92/6/9, E304200/3/5/16/21/33/5/41/8/50/7/68/74/83, E304300/1/5/7/14/5/26/9/32/6/9/46/7/51/6/9/89/91/5/7,

E304401/2/5/13/5/8/30/5/7/44/5/56/61/6/77/91-3/5, E304500/7/10/24/6/9/34/5/44/52/7/64/5/8/9/72/6 /83/4, 304604/12/5/6/9/23/32/7/43/5/55/6/9/63/70/4/7/99, E304705/14/5/20/34/47/50/66/9-72/4/5/8 /80/4/9/90, E304801/6/29/35/43-5/74/5/8/81/8/9/92, E304909/16/20/3/4/7/33/5/7/8/44/5/8/51/4/6/9/61/2 /70/5/8/9/92/5, E305001-3/6/8/9/12/5/23/9/31/3/40/3/6/7/54/6/63/7-72/5/8/82/8/91/3, E305100/8/11/20/3 /6/46/9/52/9/62/9/72/80/4/92/6, E302500-2/7/10/2/8-20/2/5/9/34/9/44/9-51/3/5/6/9/62/3/73/8/84/95/7/8, E305303/5/11/3/48/50/4/9/62-4/72/3/7/9/84/5/8/92-6, E305403/4/8/19/21/4/8/36/60/3/9/71/3/7/80/5/7/96, E305507/14/9/30/6/9/43/8-50/2/7/8/60/72/4/6/80/2-5/8/9/96/7, E305600/4/6/7/9/12-4/23/4/31/5/8/53/63/9 /72/5/7/84/7-9/94/7-9, E305708/10/3/7/20/1/9/34/8/40/4/8/50-2/65/9/72/3/5/7/9/82/5/6/90/7, E305802/5 /6/9/13/7/8/22/4/7/8/30/2-4/45/7/50/8/61/70/4/8-80/8/91/5/7, E305906-8/12/4-6/8/9/21/4-6/8-30/8/9/41/7 /8/54/62/6/7/72/4/86-8/90/1/3, E306002/4/12/4/8/20/4/5/42/4/50/2/5-8/60/2/5/72/3/82/5/8/91/6, E306101 /3-6/8/15/7/8/26/7/35/9/49/50/9/66/74/82/91/3/5/6/8, E306585/8/95/8, E306609/12/3/5-7/9/26/32/7/9/45 /9/54/6/7/9/61/6/7/70/2/5/6/81/3/6/7/90/9, E306701/4/12/9/25/6/36/9/40/3-5/7/54/64/7/74/5/82/2/4/6/8/99, E306803/5/11/3/4/21/7/37-9/42-4/56/7/65/8/70/8/80-2/93/4/7/9, E306903/8/9/18/9/21/3/4/7/36/8/9/49/54-6/8/62- 4/74/7/8/81/3/6/91-3/9, E307004-11/4/21-3/5-7/9/32-4/46/7/52/3/7/8/62/5/7/77/9/84/5/90/1/3/6, E307103/6/12- 4/21/6/9/36/7/41/8/50/6/61/2/4/78/82/94/6, E307200/4/10/5/9/31-3/8/44/6/9/54/7/8/62/ 70/1/4/6-8/81/7/90, E307301/2/7/10/3/4/7/8/21/2/9/34/6/40/3/56/72/3/5/6/9/80/2/3/90/1/4/7, E307400-2 /4/6/8/15/7/8/20/6/7/31/2/6/9/40/6/9/51/2/61/5/76/8-80/2/91-4/7, E307502/5-7/9/13/5/32/3/7/9/40/4-7 /50/1/8/64/5/70/4/7/8/84/7/93/6, E307607/12/7-22/4-6/8/30/1/6/8/9/42/6/7/50/1/5/8/60/3/4/8/70/4/6/81/7 /8/94/5/7-9, E307714/5/7/9/20/3/8/31/3/4/7/40/5/57/8/63/5/7/70/2/8/85/99, E307804/9/10/7/8/21/2/30/3 /6/8/46/8/59/64/8/9/73/4, E308136/43/9/50/5/63/81/3/90/2, E308209/13/8/22/4/5/7-9/35/6/42/60/3/4/6/9 /76/9/80/2/92/3/7/9, E308300/3/6/19/21/4/7/9/30.

B345848 taken at Okehampton, Devon in June 1981. This example is also a post-1977 rebody of the more usual welded variety and is in freight brown. It has however been condemned and this is probably due to a need for repairs rather than being surplus to requirements. (Author's Ref No W9420/DL)

Unfitted with Morton pattern brakegear and spindle buffers
B345008/21/2/5/30/51/76/85, B345101/8/15/29/36/41/8/87, B345216/44/54/98, B345315/21/55/79/80 /94/7, B345416/62, B345523/48/60/1/89, B345617/41/3/83-5/8/90/1/7, B345717/20/2/4/5/52/71/3/82/3, B345805/7/23/31/55/71/81/4, B346010/21/51/62, B346105/16/24/37/43/52/78/87, B346213/39/54/89, B346300; B413951-4/7/61-3/6/8-70/3/5/8-80/2/3/8/90/1, B41400/2/4/7-10/4/6/8/9/21/2/6/8-33/6-8/40 /2/4/6/9, B415150/8/61/3/4/7/8/70-2/9/81/3/5/8/9/92/4/7, B415202/10/2/4/5/8/9/26/8-31/3-5/8/41/7/57/8 /66/72/4/9/82/4/6/90/1/4/5, B415301/2/5/8/9/12/6/9/22/7/9/30/6-8/40/2/6/9/52/6/8/9/63/4/8/70/1/4/5/7-9 /83/4/7/96/9, B415402-4/6/10/3/4/7/8/21/6/7/9-31/3/8/9/42/4/5/9/50/2/3/61/70/4/5/88/9, B415503-5/7/12 /4/5/22/3/7/8/30/2-4/7/8/42/3/8/50/1/3-5/9/62/5/8/71/2/7/80-2/4/6/92/4-8, B415600/4/6-10/2/4/5/8/20/1/6 /7/30/1/7/9/40/7/8/50-2/4/7/8/61/3/75/81/3-6/91/3/6/7/9, B415701-3/11/20/2/4/8/9/32/6/7/42/4/7/52/3/7-9 /61/3/6/8/71/9/81/2/5-7/95-7/9, B415803/7/9/12/8/20/3/7/8/31/3/5/7/40/1/7/50/7/63/5/72/4/8/80/1/6/8/92 /5/8/9, B415905/6/8/11/2/7/8/21-3/7-9/31/4/5/40/3/7/8/50/8/63/5/9/74/6-80/7/90/3-6,

B345030 taken at Birkenhead Docks, February 1979. This chassis came originally from B417508, which was one of the rare riveted wagons with Morton pattern unfitted brakegear built to diagram 1/145. Livery was freight brown. (Author's Ref No W8229/DL)

B416002/5/8/12/9/23/31/3/4/43/50/4/61/4/5/73-5/8/83/7/90/3/4, B416100/4/5/9/13/8/9/22/32/4/42/6/7 /57/61/8-70/2/7/9/83/6/7/94-6, B416203/5/11/7/8/20/1/4-6/9-32/4/41-3/50/2/5/6/60/4/6-8/71-4/6/80/3 /8/9/92/5-7, B416300/13/8/23/5/6/30/2/4/5/40-3/9/50/4/5/9/67/9/70/4/6/81/3/5-7/96/7, B416400-3/6/8 /10/5-7/20/2/3/6/7/9/39/43/4/8/9/52/61/7/9/72/4/7/80/5-7/92/3, B416501/4/5/9/10/2/4/6/36-8/42/7/9/52 /72/4/5/7/80/1/6/96/9, B416602/3/7/17/22/5/6/8/32/5/6/54/5/67/72/3/5/6/9/83/7/93, B416701/4/6/9/13 /21/7/9/35/6/9/49/59/60/7/8/75/6/8/85/8/90/2/5, B416806/13/6/20/1/8/33/46/54/6/7/62/3/70/1/86/7/91/6 /8, B416906/25/34/5/7/42/5/7/50/3/4/8/70/81/5/91/2/5/7, B417003/11/2/5/22/3/39/41/50/5/8/62/76-8/80 /1/6/9/92/5, B417101/9/12/5-7/21/2/6/7/30/2/4/9/46/8/9/52-4/6/65/7/73/5/8/9/91/3/5, B417200/1/4/5/10/3 /5-8/21/6/7/31-4/6/7/9/42/51/4/7/8/60/1/3/5-8/72/5/7/9/80/9/94/8, B417306/12/6/21/4/8/9/34/5/42/5/6/50 /8/61/2/6/70/3/7/9/81/2/94-6, B417400/3-6/8/10/4/5/23/6/7/30/2/4/8/9/43/6-8/51/5/6/60/1/3/4/6/8/71/2/4 /9/81/7/8/90/3, B417504/6/11/4/5/7/9/20/3/5/6/8/31/5/9/42/9-51/3/8/60-2/6/8/70/3/8/84/6/97/9, B417600 /1/6/7/9/11-4/6-21/5-8/38/9/41/3-6/9/52/61/2/4/8/71/2/7/84/6-8/91/3/6, B417700/2/6/7/11/4-8/20/2/3/8 /32/5-7/40/2/4/5/8/51/4-6/66/7/9-72/4/80/1/4/6/8/94/5/7, B417800/7/8/11-4/7/9/21/3/6/7/9/30/41/3/5/8 /50/3/9/61/2/7/8/70/3/5/8-80/3/5/91/3/6/9, B417906-8/12/4/5/9-21/7-30/3/5/9-45/8/51/3/61/3-5/76/8-81 /4/7-9/93/4/6, B41800/8-10/6/9/23/5/31/8/43/6-9/53/8/66/9/70/4/9/80/6/9/92-4/7, B418101/3/6/11/4/7/9 /21/2/7/30/1/5/7/9/44/7/9/52/4/6/60-5/7/8/71/2/8/82/5-7/9-91/8/9, B418200/5/10/2/3/6/9/20/4/33/4/7/8 /43/5/6/50/6/7/61/71/3/9/84/8/90/2/3, B418302/3/5/7/8/14/20/2/3/38/50/65/6/70/8/80/1/5/92, B418400-3 /7/15/7/8/20/40/6/7/52/5/8/9/61/3/7/71/3/6/80/94, B418504-6/14/22/4/5/30/5/6/9/46/56/63/8/9/79/87/90, B418600/1/4/5/15/20/6/33/40/3/5/6/9/50/3/8/62/4/5/72/5/7/84/9/91/9, B418706/7/10/23/33/44/6/7/9/50/ 7/69/73/5/9/87/93/9, B418801/9/13/4/8/24/8/30-3/40/2/5/7/50/6/61/2/7/71/5/8/88/93-5/7/9, B418901/2 /4/5/7/12/21/34/5/40/1/5/8/52/3/5/6/62/4/6/8/73/82/7/91/2/6/8, B419004/6/16/26/9/30/3-6/54/62-4/6/7 /70/6/8/82/5/6/92/9, B419113/4/7/21/4/6/8-30/3/6/55/60/2/71/82/91/4, B419214/6/50/66/7/78-80/6/90, B419301/6/8/12/7/23/36/44/5/53/60/1/74/7/8/82/4/7/92/9, B419401/3/5/7/10-3/5/20/39/53/5/71/5/81/92 /6/7, B419500/4/14/20-2/34/45/9/65/72/4/6/7/84-6/9/92/7/8, B419600-3/14/20/7-9/38/44/7/50/4/6/8/61 /3/9/73/80/3/9/91, B419712/3/5/24/5/9/31/3/45/6/59/60/4/80/3/6, B419810/5/6/22/8/33/43/5/6/9/50/5/7 /62/6/78/83/8/90/7, B419917/23/9/30/48/9/51/3/63/73/6/88/91/5, B420001/4/5/8/10/1/4/6/7/9/21/7/8 /33/6/8/41-3/9-51/5/7/60/7/70/5/83/6/97, B420101/7/8/10-3/24/6/7/31/8-40/9/53/60/3/72/86/7/95/6, B420200/6/14/8/21/30/1/4/40/3/51/9/61/4/5/71/4/6-8/87/9, B420300/1/4/7/13/6/9-21/4-7/30/4/5/41/6 /52/3/5/7/69/72/4/80/2/4/92/3/6, B420400/3/6/8/14/6-8/24/5/8/35/40/4/8/50/3/5/9/64/5/9/72/5/6/82/90 /5/7/9, B420500/4/9/12/7/25/30/4/45/56/65/71/7/8/83/8-90/5/7, B420600/2/11/3/7/8/26/7/9/32/3/6/8 /42/3/7/50/7/60/5/6/8/74/7/80/2/6/9/92/3/5/8, B420701/4/6/9/14/26/8/52-4/65/6/77/9/98, B420800/3/7 /10/3/36/41/4/7/52/8/62/4/6/7/9/75/7/9/84/93, B420906/11/4/5/8/9/21/39/41/59/62/78, B421012/3/7/30 /43/5/50/61/4/74/5/80/90-2/5, B421101/7/13/4/7/21/4/38/44/7/52/8/60/1/7/8/78/81/2/4/5/93, B421204 /5/7/11/4/9/20/5/30/2/8/47/51/2/9/60/4/8/71/7/81/8/9/93-5/9, B421303/5/11/20/2/3/34/8/41/9/53/70/80 /2/97, B421405/7/15/42/7/62/70/80/9/90, B421502/44/53/67, B421626/54/8/93, B421750/90, B421808 /11/3-5/27/8/32/5/42/51/67/74/87/9/90/4, B421915/49/80/5/8/90, B422015/38/42/58, B422115/36/45/7, B422200/18/28/54/75/6/81, B422300/4/10/3/4/20/6/31/3/7/40/50/3/6/62/71/80/94/8,

B422407/12/44/51/3/7/65/7/73-6/9/80/4/94/8/9, B422502/11/2/4/5/9/20/3/5/31/8/9/42/3/50/2/6/8/9/61/3/7
/70/3/7/9/81/3/4/6/8-90/7/9, B422602/9/12/3/20/2/4/30/4/6/7/9/47/8/53/4/6/9/63/6/7/9/71-6/9/85-91/3,
B422700/2/5/6/8/11/3/5/8/9/21/3/4/7/8/33-40/2-4/6-9, B423059/61/5/73/4/6/9/80/4/8/9, B423113/7/21/50
/62/3/7/70/5/8/86/94, B423201/9/33/5/50/3/7/9/69/83/7/91/4, B423300/2/6/7/11/2/6-8/21/4/5/9/38/40/8
/53/4/7/66/70/1/6/83/98, B423404/10/6/8/23/30/2/-5-7/9/42/4/50/1/63/4/6/79/91/5/7, B423511/8/23/37/8
/50/67/9/70/9/80/8/93/5, B423603/4/11/7/23/5/8/30/3-5/40/50/1/3/61/7/75/80/1/94/7/8, B423702/7/14/8
/28/34/6/9/44/7/52/9/61/4/5/9/71/3/4/7/80/6/92-4/7, B423803/7/11/5/8/22/7/40/2/3/52/60/7/77/8/82/6/8
/94/8, B423901/7/15/20/7/46/9/57/61-3/6/72/3/82/4/6/9, B424000/2/9/12-5/29/34/5/45/50/4/8/64/5/8/9
/71/3/5/81/8/92, B424100/4/5/7/10/4/7/22/6-8/30/6/46/8/52/5/7/8/63/9/75/89/94/7, B424200/14/21/4/6/9
/30/6/41/8/56/7/65-7/74-6/89/91/3/5/7, B424306/7/17/30/75/85/7/9/93, B424401/18/9/23/6/32/5/6/43/8
/51/9/67/8/72/9, B424502/6/9/15/7/9/21/2/6/7/32/3/42/4/7/54/5/8-60/3/5/70/1/4/6/8/9/82/4/9/96/9,
B424604/13/5/7/9/21/6/8/33/8/50/7/61/3/6/79/80/4/6/90/2-4, B424701/2/4-6/13/23/4/32/7/57/8/60/2/9
/72/8-81/94, B424803/5/6/8/11/4-6/8/22-6/39/42/8/50/2/5/6/69/73/5/88-90/2/8, B424904/7/12-4/8/20/3/9
/37/40/2/6/8/50/8/9/61/8/9/73/4/8/9/82/92/4/6, B425001/2/15-7/22/9/33/5/8/40/1/6/51/5/7/8/60/4/8/72/4
/84/5/8/93, B425108-10/5/20/3/8/34/5/40/4/9/50/9/62/6/7/76/9/82/90-2/6/7, B425200/2/5/9/24/7-9/34/7/8
/41/2/6/9/56/64/6/74/9/84/90, B425311/2/5/7/9/21/5/6/31/3-7/42/4/6/55/60-2/4/5/9/73/4/9/84/92,
B425406/11/7/24/7/41/4-6/52/7/66/9/70/3/7/8/83/96, B425512/21/5/30/2/4/44/60/8/72/3/7-9/97, B425609
/27/43/5/78, B425713/5/9-21/5/33/40/5/53/60/6/9/73/87/90/2/7/9, B425806/13/7/8/24/39/41/7/8/61/4/5
/76/86/90/2/3/6/9, B425902-4/13/25/7/57/65-7/77/97/9, B426004/8/9/20/6/32/43/55/67/8/73/8/82/3/91,
B426104/7/10/3/28/30/41/50/6/8/63/5/7/95/7, B426200/6/16-8/25/7/33/40/1/7/53/7/9/63/9/81/95/6,
B426304/16/29/33/68/79/92, B426406/18/20/41/2/8/73/7/83/92, B426505/18/28/31/4/9/58/62-4/70-2/4
/7/9/84/5/8, B426609/10/6/8/20/8/30/8/41/3/57/8/69/72/5/7/85/9/94/7, B426731/42/9/50/5/7/62/3/7/81/4
/8/98, B426804/5/9/13/5/7/8/41/3/65/70-3/93/9, B426900/7/9/19/21/3/7/31/42/3.

Right: B417243 taken at Strood, Kent in November 1974. This chassis is from the rare riveted diagram 1/145 and resembles a riveted vehicle in the rebuilt form with Huck bolts. Livery was rail grey with HOP 21 code and metric tare. (Author's Ref No W5107/DL)

Below: B418536 taken at Toton Yard in August 1980. Based on a diagram 1/146 chassis, this vehicle is also in rail grey livery with later HTO code and metric tare. (Author's Ref No W8181/DL)

B424608 taken at Mottram Yard in February 1977. This was another diagram 1/146 chassis rebodied in the early rail grey period and, in this case, has been fitted with roller bearings. Code is HOP 21 and metric tare. (Author's Ref No W5893/ DL)

<u>Unfitted with Morton pattern brakegear, roller bearings and self-contained buffers</u>
B345001, B345148/87, B345298, B345446/58/64/5/9/72/3/6/92, B345548, B345604/13/4/50/1, B345771/56/80/7, B345855/71/81; B426967/75/91, B427020/54/64/6, B427104/11/8/20/8/33/7/49/50/2/5 /71/3/7/9/81-3/9, B427202/11/2/6/26/9/38/47/59/61/70/1/80/2, B427303/15/21/38/43/6/8/61/5/82/5/95, B427409/12/4/20/33/8/42/5/55/62/5/6/8/73, B427504/8/12/9/24/5/39/41/54/60/6/7/73/9/81/2/4/92/7, B427608/10/5/6/28/32/7/41/8/9/55/9/61/3/74/82/6/7/95/8, B427708/18/22/3/9-31/5/50/1/4/5/8/62/8/71/3 /83/9/92/6/7, B427800/3/4/11/3/9/21/6/9/31/2/48/55/7/68/71/3-5/9/82/9/94/7/9, B427900/3/4/8/9/13/5 /32/7/43/62/72/4/82/3/6/94, B428000/8/16/25/40/1/3/4/6/8/66/7/70/81/2/6/7, B428103/4/14/5/21/4/45/8/9 /51/6/68/70/5/8/84-7/97, B428209/22/8/30/30/4/65/7/73/8/87, B428312/3/5/27/8/41/53/9/61/7/74 /81/3/6/8/91, B428404/6/9-12/4/6/9/26/9-31/4/6/41/4/7/9/51/4/6/7/9/67/71/2/6-8/83/9/90/3, B428501/42 /59/64/7/8/76/81/94-6/8, B428600/4/13/4/7/9/20/3/5/7/39/46/53/5-7/62/4/7/72-9/81/7/90/2/8, B428700-3/5-7/11-6/9/23/6/30/2/4/5/40/5/53/4/63/4/6/7/9/71/5/80/90/5/8, B428801/4/5/9/14/6/24/7/8/36/9/44/61/3-5/9/73/4/92/7/8, B428903/5/7/10-3/5/6/8-22/38/44/5/7/8/50/1/5/8/62/3/5-8/70/4-7/9/82/3/5/91/4/8, B429000/1/3-8/10/1/3/8/22/3/5/8-31/3-7/9-41/3/6/7/9.

B427686 taken at Ripple Lane, East London in April 1980. This is based on one of the later chassis and had roller bearings from new, although the buffers may have been changed at some stage. Livery is rail grey with HTO code and metric tare. (Author's Ref No W8197/DL)

Unfitted with Morton pattern brakegear, roller bearings and OLEO hydraulic buffers
B345000/2/3/6/12/23/6/47/8/66/72/7, B345109/18/20/3/58/81, B345228/39/58/66, B345314/58/9, B345408/25/42/48/64/5/9/72/3/6/92, B345516, B345604/13/4/50/1, B345841/6/80/7, B345928/51/68, B346030/1; B429903/5/8/12/4/5/9/21/9/31/6/46/50/1/6/8/62/4/5/70/6/86/8/96/7, B430009/16/24-7/32/4 /40/1/3/6/50/6/9/61/4/5/72/4/6/7/80/6/8/91/7, B430100/9/11/22/5-9/31/8-42/7-9/52/4/7/60/1/3/5/6/8/75/6 /82/4/6/8/93/5/6/9, B430208/9/12/3/6/20/1/4/6/9/31/5/9/42/3/5/58/60/4/7/9/74/9/82/7/9/91/2/4/5/8, B430303/7/8/15/9/23/8/9/31/2/6/40/2/4/7/63/73/8/88/96/7, B430402/5/6/9/10/23/5/7/41/4/8/53/5/63/9/77 /83/92/5/8, B430504/7/13/24/7/45/57/8/65/73/5/87/91/6, B430604/24/6/8/30/46-8/51-3/5/65/7/70/9/84-7 /9/94-6, B430701/2/10/4/5/22/3/5-7/31/3/5/7/40/53/5/8/61/9/79-81/5/91/2/5/9, B430800/2/3/9/14/8/25/31 /6/53/72/80/7/90, B430908/13/22/36/8/41/5/6/58/9/64/72/80/7/91, B431066/81/8, B431105/7/9/14/9 /21/3/6/33/7/8/42/50/3/60/8/78/81/3/7/9, B431205/14/30/2/4/42/7/9/51/7/61/8/70/1/8/83/8, B431309/19/ 34/7/40/1/50/60/72/82/90/1/9, B431411/22/33/41/50/3/8/62/5/82, B431515/22/5/35/57/61/4/79/92/3, B431605/11/2/4-6/9/25/6/31/5/43/7/53/69/75/86, B431714/57/8/67/8/73/82/3/90, B431802/6/26/34-6 /52/3/68/70/80/90, B431900/8/10/2/4/24/5/40/62/8/74-6/9/81/8/92/5, B432000/19/25/7/8/31/3/4/42/4/50 /76/81/91/5, B432100/7/25/6/40/4/55/8/60/3/78/81/3/5, B432206/27/9/33/40/53/63/8, B432304/21/5/39 /42/3/7/54/5/69/77-9, B432401/5/7/15/20/32/3/6/8/46/8/9/56/9/65/8/74-6/85/92, B432502/5/7/22/6/31/6 /56/69/71/5/81/3/95, B432601/19/21/42/50/3/5/66/8/72/80/1/6/7, B432709/16/20/9/34/7/9/44/50/5/82/90, B432808/15/21/2/4/41/50/72/6/9/83/5/8/92, B432916/24/7/8/40/6/8/63/5/80/99, B433003/10/3/22/30/43 /53/5/83/90/8, B433116/22/7/40/8/54/9/69/70/7/99, B433209/26/7/39/98/9, B433303/7/28/38/42/4/8/61 /83/3/5, B433403/16/33/42/8/9/63/7/9/78/88.

B431242 taken at Whitehaven, Cumbria in October 1977. This is based on one of the final diagram 1/149 chassis and had roller bearings from new with spindle buffers. Livery is freight brown with HTO code and metric tare. (Author's Ref No W6658/DL)

Vacuum-braked vehicles with new bodywork, apart from those rated at 25 Tonnes and numbered in the B340000 to B340924 series, all came from the later batches with Morton brakegear, and a considerable number of formerly unfitted wagons were vacuum-braked when in rebodied condition. It is not known whether this occurred at the time of rebodying or earlier. Numbers of those retaining 21.5 Tonne rating after rebodying were as follows:

B413967/72/6/85/92, B414011/2, B415152/76/80/7, B415208/16/37/43/4/52/69/80/96/9, B415318/23/5 /31/5/9/44/50/86/9/90/2/3, B415045/40/1/6/8/51/5/84/5/90-3/7, B415500/2/11/9/20/5/52/8/61/3/6/9/76/ 90/1, B415605/28/9/34/41/6/9/59/69/71/89, B415714/30/3/8/41/3/64/5/9/84/9/92-4, B415811/7/32/8/49 /51/2/9/68/90/7, B415907/25/30/3/42/51/6/66/8/71/5/97/8, B416003/10/8/28/41/2/6/53/6/8/67/8/92/8, B416108/10/1/7/29/33/6/45/8/55/6/60/2/5-7/74/80/1/9/93/7/9, B416215/9/28/40/53/9/84, B416301/2/6/8 /11/5/45/8/52/63/4/72/93/5, B416405/19/55/7/62/6/82-4, B416500/11/3/9/25/7/31/2/4/9/40/3-5/50/8/61/4,

B415224 taken at Hoo Junction, Rochester in October 1974. This was originally an unfitted vehicle and has received vacuum-brakegear but retained oil axleboxes. Code is HOP 21 VB and livery is freight brown. Tare deleted. (Author's Ref No W4683/DL)

B416570/82/94, B416605/6/9/12/5/37/40/6/9/60/8/80/90/1/7/9, B416700/2/3/14/20/2/4/30/2/3/40/1/6/7, B417554/7/64/5/80/9/98, B417615/24/30/4/57/74/8/98/9, B417705/12/24/41/64/78/93/8, B417833/7/49 /54/64/74/82/6, B417923/6/32/8/47/52/7/8/68/9/75/7, B418003/6/15/37/50-2/5/6/72/5/82/3/91/5, B418102/4/5/7/10/29/41/2/5/50/70/5/6/88/96, B418202/4/9/11/25/30/44/9/53/4/66/7/74/5/80/3/7/97/9, B418300/12/6/7/9/21/31/40/8/52-4/7/63/4/71/3/9/905, B418405/14/6/27/35/8/41/50/1/6/72/85/91/6, B418507-9/13/5/21/8/37/8/43-5/50/2/5/72/5/82/94/8, B418610/9/34/41/51/2/60/6/7/9/73/80/1/5/8/92/3/8, B418703/9/13-5/8/22/5/8/31/5/6/40/2/3/52/8/60/2/5/6/70/1/8/80/2/8/90/7, B418803-5/7/11/6/7/9/20/2/6/7 /34/44/9/52/4/5/9/63/9/79/84/9/91, B418906/14/26/37/8/47/59/61/3/76/84/6/8/93, B419003/7-9/13/4/21/3 /37/40/9/53/7/8/65/83/4/9-91/7, B419101/8/20/31/2/4/8/9/47/9/51/6/63/70/3/5/6/9/81/3/5/9/92/9, B419200/8/9/21/3/8/35/9/42/51/60/70/1/3/83/8/92, B419304/9/13/9/26-30/2/4/55/62-5/8/9/71/2/9/86/8 /90/4, B419408/9/16/9/22/31/3/4/8/50/2/66/9/79/86/91/3, B419506-8/10/2/5/6/23/5-7/37-9/44/7/8/51/3/6 /61/6/71/82/3/7/91, B419611/22/36/49/53/60/70/6/7/84/8/97, B419706/26-8/32/5/8/42/7/50-2/5/6/66/8 /70/2/3/87/90/4/6, B419807/9/12/7/23-5/34/8/41/52/4/6/73/80/1/5/95/8, B419902/6/14/8/20/2/4/36/40/2/4 /52/8/61/2/5/7/70/4/8/9/82/3/5/7/9/90/3/6/7, B420002/7/15/8/23-5/31/5/44/7/8/68/9/71/4/8/80/1/5/98, B420105/14/22/3/42/7/8/50/66/70/4/8/80/9/93, B420201/8/9/11/20/7/9/33/6/9/41/2/55/7/8/68/9/75/9 /86/96/7, B420303/6/12/44/50/1/9/60/2/4/73/9/85/9, B420405/7/9/13/9/23/7/36/42/63/74/7/9/83/7-9 /93/4/6, B420503/10/26/33/6/9/41/6/9/51/8/9/61/74/9/80/2/5/7/92/3/8, B420608/10/2/4/20/2/3/5/35/7/46 /72/8/9/87, B420700/5/10/7/9/21-4/32/3/6/7/44/9/58/63/8/71-4/85/6/90/9, B420801/4/5/9/11/9/20/6/33 /7-40/2/8/59/61/5/70/1/3/8/83/8/92/4/7, B420901/9/16/7/22/4/6/8/9/31/3/40/5/8/9/52-4/6/8/61/70/2/3/6 /80/3/91, B421001/2/4/5/14/6/8/22-5/7/33/7/40/4/53/5-7/65/9/71/6=8/81/4/7/9/93/7, B421103/8/11/8-20 /6/9-33/9/66/75/9/80/8/90/6, B421201/9/10/5/21/7/34/6/9/41/4/56/62/5/74/80/91, B421300/6/9/18/25/37 /59/66/86/92/3/5/8, B421400/8-11/6/7/23/4/30/2/6/7/40/6/9/52/4/6/9/65/6/8/73/6/8/9/83/6/8/92/3/7, B421504/5/7/8/11/4/6/7/20-2/4/5/7-9/32/3/7/40/7/9-52/61/3/4/72/7/85/8/90/5/9, B421600/1/4/12/3/5/7 /21-4/8/34/6/7/44/5/7/8/66/74/7/81/5/6/90/6/9, B421703/8/9/14/6/20/3/5/9/30/3/4/40/6/54/61-3/6/9/72/3/6 /86/9/92-6/9, B421801/7/20/33/4/6/9/43-6/9/50/2/3/5/61/6/75/9/81/3/4/96-9, B421902/3/5/6/9/16/8/9 /22/5/7/9/32/3/5/8/46/7/50/3-5/60/6/7/77/81/3/99, B422002/8-10/2/6/8/20/2/6/7/33/5/43/4/6/9/52/61/4/9 /72/4/8-80/2-4/8/90/1/6/7, B422103-5/7/11/2/4/6/8/9/22-4/7/8/34/7/8/48/51/2/62/4/74/8/83/4/6/7/99, B422203/7/23/6/7/9/31/3/5/6/8/9/43/5/7/8/52/6/63/7/8/72/80/2/4/6/90/9, B422301-3/7/15/8/9/21/7/8/30/9 /45/7/63/4/9/72/4/6/84/9/96, B422400/1/4/6/10/3/6/7/9/20/4-6/8/30/5/45/7-9/52/4-6/8-60/4/6/9/78/83/5/7 /90/5, B422501/3/4/9/10/26/7/30/3/4/40/54, B422605/8, B422722, B423050/1/5/60/70/1/7/8/81/3/6 /91/5/6, B423102/6/10/8/22-4/8/9/32-5/8-43/7/51-3/5/7/9/69/77/80/2/3/8/91, B423200/4-7/10-2/5/7/9 /26/30/9/41/2/5/8/52/5/6/62-4/7/70-4/8/9/81/2/5/8/90, B423304/5/8/15/26/7/31/2/9/45/6/9/51/5/6/8/60-2 /7/73/7/80/1/5/6/8/92-6, B423401/3/7/13/4/7/24/6/9/31/4/40/1/6/52/9/60/2/5/9/72/7/87-90, B423501/5/7 /13/6/24/8/30/40/3/4/7/54/8/62/6/72/3/83/5/7/98/9, B423600-2/7/12/3/9/22/9/31/6/44/5/7/52/4-7/60/2/ 70/3/6-8/89/90/2/6/9, B423709/12/3/9/23-6/31/5/7/40/2/3/8/51/6/63/6/83/5/7/90/5/6, B423828/32/3/6/8 /44/6-50/3/6/7/61/8/9/74/81/4/7/97, B423900/8/13/23/5/30/2/3/7/44/7/52/3/68-71, B424024,

B416480 taken at Strood, Kent in August 1979. This example was unfitted when rebodied but has been fitted with vacuum brakegear subsequently. Livery is rail grey with HTV code and metric tare on freight brown panel. (Author's Ref No W7777/ DL)

B424206/10/5/8/22/31/43/5/7/9/51/4/5/8-60/2/4/9/80/4/96/8, B424300-2/5/9/12-4/20/1/4/7-9/32/4/5/41/2
/6/52/4/5/9/96/71/6/7/9/81/3/90/2/6/8/9, B424403/6/7/13/5/22/7/9/30/3/4/8/9/45/7/52/3/7/8/61/3/71/6/8
/85/6/8/9/95/7, B414501/8/11/2/6/8/34/5/41/6/50/1/3/7/62/6/77/93-5/8, B424601/6/7/9/16/22/3/30/1/4/7
/41/4/51/2/4-6/67/70/1/5/7/88/91/7, B424703/8/11/4/7/9/20/5/30/3/8-40/3/7/50/2/5/6/9/63/71/3-5/7/83
/93/7/8, B424804/19/28/30/3/4/6/41/7/57/60-2/4/5/77/9/84/94/7/9, B424908/9/15/7/21/30/1/9/45/9/51/2
/4-6/70/89/90/8, B425009/12/4/32/44/5/52/6/9/61/2/7/9/77/86/9/92/6/7, B425100/3/4/6/14/6-8/21/4/7
/30/2/6-9/42/6-8/54/7/8/69/70/7/81/4/98, B425203/7/10-2/4/5/7/22/6/30/1/9/40/3-5/8/52-4/7/8/62/3/5/8
/78/85/6/8/9/92/3/8/9, B425300/6/13/6/22/39/48/56/7/9/63/81/9/91/3, B425402/4/7/13/6/22/30/7/9/40/55
/64/71/5/6/85/7/8/90-3/9, B425503/6/7/9-11/6-8/26/35/7/8/40/2/3/6/8/50-2/5/62/5/7/70/4/5/81/3/5/6/9
/95/8/9, B425601/4/10/2-4/7/9/21/2/4/9/31/4/9/44/6/8-50/2/5/60/3/6/70/4/9/85/91/9, B425700-2/4/6/9/14
/28/9/32/4/7/41/51/4/6/62/3/5/7/8/71/4/6/9-81/3/6/8/95/6/8, B425800/8-12/22/5/7/8/32/4/7/8/40/4/5/9
/50/2/7/9/73/8/82/3/94, B425900/1/8/9/17/8/22/31/5/9/41/50/5/62/3/8/9/71/2/6/9/84/7/90/2/4/6/8,
B426003/5/7/11-6/8/9/21/3/4/30/1/4/5/7/8/40-2/4/5/50/60/2-6/9/74/5/7/80/5-7/90/2/4/6/8/9, B426100/3
/5/9/12/24/31/7/8/42-5/57/9/68/9/71/7/81-6/8/91/6, B426202/3/8-10/3/20/2/3/30/1/6/8/9/43/5/6/8/9
/71/3/8/9/83-5/8/92-4/7/9, B426301/5/7/11/2/4/5/9/21/3/5-8/30/4/5/40/4/7/8/52/6-8/60/1/3/4/70/3/4/6
/85/7/90/4/5/7/9, B426401/7/8/11/3/4/6/9/22-5/7/9/31/2/5/7/8/43-5/7/9-52/4-9/61/4/6/7/9-71/84-8/91/8,
B426500/3/9/12/3/5/7/9/20/2/5/9/32/3/6/40/3/4/7/9/52/6/7/66/8/73/8/81/6/9/90/4/7, B426602/3/6/8/19
/25/9/31/3/5-7/9/45/6/54/6/9/60/2-5/7/8/74/8/80/2/3/91/5/6/9, B426701/2/4/6/9/11/6/7/21/2/4-6/8/9
/32-4/8/43/7/51/2/4/6/9/72-6/8/80/2/90/4, B426801/3/6/7/14/9/21-3/7/31/3/6/9/44/6/8/50-2/4/6-8/61/3
/6-9/77/80/3-5/7/94/7/8, B426901-6/10/1/4/7/8/22/8/9/35/7/8/44-8/69, B427034/44, B427161/93,
B427210/28/43/55/86, B427319/31/59, B427400-4/10/5/6/30/4-6/9/40/3/4/6/52/4/7/61/70/5/6/8-80/3-6
/8/90-2/7/9, B427501/5/6/9/14/20/2/3/8/9/34/5/7/49/55/61/4/5/8/70/4/7/8/85/91/4/5/8, B427602/14/7
/9-21/4/35/6/9/45-7/53/7/8/62/5/8-70/8/81/4/5/8/92/4, B427700/1/3/5/10/1/6/33/8/9/42/5/61/3/5/9/70/4
/6/9/80/2/91/4/5/8, B427808/9/15/8/20/2/4/33/5/7/9/43-5/50/2/4/9-62/4/7/9/77/8/85/6/92,
B427902/11/2/4/24/8/33/4/46/9/50/4/5/7/63/8/75/8/9/85/7/92/3/7/9, B428001/2/6/11-5/7/21/3/32-4/6/9/
50/2/3/8/62/5/78/89/97, B428106-8/10/1/6/8/20/2/3/6/31/5/46/7/50/2/4/66/7/73/89/90/4/6/8, B428200/2
/3/10/3/8/24/5/32/5-8/43-6/8/51/8/63/6/8/9/74-6/81/2/4/8/94/5/8, B428301-4/6/11/6/7/9/20/2-6/32/4/46
/7/9/93, B428439/99, B428509/50/4/7/8/65/9/82/3/6/8/93, B428606/7/9-11/6/8/21/4/9/32/3/7/8/42/5/
51/8/9/61/8/91/6/9, B428737/8/41/3/9/58/60/72/81/6, B428817/20/31/2/7/40/2/3/5-8/50/1/5/8/62/8/76/8
/85/8/93, B428909/17/26/8/9/31/2/4/5/43/52/3/6/9/61/78/84/7/93/6/7/9, B429009/12/4/5/26/7/42/4, B429355/7-
9/62/5/7/72/9/84/9/95/9, B429400/4/10/3/6/21/3/4/7/39/41/2/5/50/2/5/6/63/6/7/70/4/90, B429500/2-
5/8/18/22/3/32/6/42/3/6/7/53-6/8/9/70/3/9/83/8/94/6, B429606/8/9/12/3/7/20/4/30/2/3/9
/43/4/9/50/3/6-9/62/70-2/5/82/7/8/92, B429700/9/14/6/9/27/31/3-6/8/9/41/7/50/2/4/8/60/1/4-6/78/80
/3-5/7/92/3/6, B429810/7/8/21/4/31/2/6/8/40/56/63/5/7/78/97, B430650, B430806/26/8/33/7/41/57/69
/92/4/6, B430902/17/21/8/48/63/70/5/94, B431003/7/19/23/34/43/68/71/86, B431116/32/44/57/8/67/72
/80/2/99, B431202/4/17/8/35/6/9/41/5/8/63/74/91, B431308/12/4/7/20/9/35/43/9/56/62/75/7/83, B431417
/8/25/6/9/44/5/57/63/81/6/92/3/6/8, B431504-7/10/2/32/43/6/7/50/4/75/8/80/3-5/9/94, B431600/13/22/33
/41/50/5/6/81/4, B431707/19/24/52/5/61/74/7/86, B431804/9/10/6/7/20/8/45/50/4/9/60/2/4/73/8/82/94/7,

B428339 taken at Barrow-in-Furness in October 1982. This is a well-weathered vacuum-braked wagon originally unfitted with a blanked-off vacuum-pipe. It was an early rebody and has a curious HTV21VB code and metric tare. (Author's Ref No W12288/DL)

B431901-3/6/15/7/8/39/46/59/64/72/82/9/96, B432013/22/4/6/37/8/51/9/61/3/4/7/9/85/90/6, B432103/4 /17/20/3/7/31/41/5/8/54/61/7/77/82/4/90/3/6/9, B432203/9/11/8/9/25/6/32/41/3-5/52/8/65/7/74/82-4/6/91, B432305/11/4/6/9/20/2/7/31/2/46/51/2/6/7/61/3/8/70/2/6/80-2/5/90/2/7-9, B432400/2/6/13/6/7/9/22/3/7/8 /31/40/1/52/4/8/64/6/73/8/81/3/9/93/5/6, B432500/1/11/4/9/20/2/4/5/7/9/34/7-9/44/51/2/4/8/9/61/5/70/7 /80/2/9/96, B432603/4/7/8/10/2/5/7/20/2/4/7/31/7/8/40/3/7-9/54/6/61/5/7/70/3/4/8/9/85/8/93/6, B432700 /1/10/2/3/5/7/24/7/41/8/51/4/7/8/61-4/6/9/72/84/5/9/93, B432801/5/6/10/1/4/28/9/32/4/6/9/40/5/55/8/62-4 /94/7, B432900/3/5/8/10/2/21/2/5/9/30/3/7/9/47/50/2/7/60-2/6/71/3/9/83/4/9/95/8, B43302/5/6/8/9/14-6 /21/3/5/6/31/5-7/40/1/4/9/50/9/66/71-4/6/7/9/85/9/99, B433108/14/5/23-5/9/31/42-4/9/53/60/5/7/8/75/6/9 /81/8/92/3, B433202/5-8/13/6/7/20/8/34/5/43/6/8/55-7/9/61/2/9/74/5/80/8, B433300/1/10/5/8/23/32/41/51 /3-5/7/63/4/8-70/6/80/1/4/5/97, B433402/6/15/21/3/7/30/2/5/41/3/7/50-4/7/60/1/4-6/76/9/83/5/9/99, B433502- 4/8/11/20/3/7/8/34/7/9/42/4/8/9/51/68/70/4/81/3/5/90/4, B433603/7/11/2/6/21/34/44/6/7/9/56 /61/6/74/6, B433702/4/7/13/5/23/7/33/6/9/43/4/7/9.

It is almost certain that there were other rebodied vehicles above and beyond those listed in this section. Reporting to BRB Headquarters at Derby was not always carried out accurately and this was the location that I copied my records, rather than the works.

Most of the unfitted wagons were withdrawn during the mid-1980s. Many of the vacuum-braked vehicles were converted to CLAM, RUDD and TOPE ballast wagons and will be dealt with in a future volume in this series.

B433037 taken at Hoo Junction, Rochester in April 1981. This wagon is a fairly early Huck bolt variant seen in weathered condition with HTO code and metric tare. (Author's Ref No W9404/ DL)

Carflats and MTV Sand Wagons

The final Carflat wagons were built during the review period. Numbers were as follows:

B745000 to B745056 CARFLAT (diagram 1/088)	11/1968 to 9/1969	3679 BR (St Rollox)	Air-braked
B745057 to B745061 CARFLAT (diagram 1/134)	8/1970 to 9/1970	3715 BR (Barassie)	Vacuum
B745062 to B745073 CARFLAT (diagram 1/137)	3/1971 to 4/1971	3757 BR (Barassie)	Vacuum
B745074 to B745087 CARFLAT (diagram 1/137)	5/1971 to 6/1971	3758 BR (Barassie)	Vacuum
B745088 to B745227 CARFLAT	7/1974 to 11/1975	3831 Various works	Vacuum
B745228 to B745297 CARFLAT	11/1974 to 5/1975	3867 BR (Swindon)	Vacuum
B745298 to B745302 CARFLAT	6/1975 to 7/1975	3868 BR (Swindon)	Vacuum

The majority of the vacuum-braked vehicles were eventually given air through-pipes and were coded FVX. These vehicles were regular used on passenger Motorail services. When these ceased, they were used to carry new road vehicles until withdrawal in the mid-1980s.

B745042 taken at Lowton St. Marys, Lancashire in August 1970. When in Motorail service, the livery was rail blue with an appropriate nameplate for the service in white, black and red. Tare weight is not legible. (Author's Ref No W2439/DL)

An interesting new type, the 24.5 Tonne MTV aggregate wagon, was introduced during the mid-1970s. These were rebuilds by Standard Wagon Co. on redundant late-1950s railtank chassis with sturdy box bodies without doors. Numbers were as follows:

B390000 to B390149 24.5t MINERAL (MTV)	6/1974 to 1/1976	3859 Standard Wagon	Vacuum

Load usually carried included large rocks, granite chippings and other mineral loads that were unloaded by grab. Some also appeared in later years loaded with sand.

In due course, they were transferred to the civil engineers fleet as ZANDER wagons and will be dealt with in the appropriate volume.

B390006 taken at Brixton, South East London in January 1980. This example is the end vehicle of a rake of MTV wagons carrying granite rocks for the Thames Flood Barrier scheme. Livery is freight brown with full pool number panel and STONE symbol on the right-hand end, not carried by the other two wagons visible. (Author's Ref No W8537/DL)

B390038 taken at Warrington (Arpley) in February 1982. This MTV wagon has seen much service and has very little lettering beyond the code box and the very small POOL 5019 train number. Livery is freight brown. (Author's Ref No W11284/ DL)

B390110 taken at Peak Forest, Derbyshire in August 1980. This view shows a distant rake of MTV wagons, with B390110 as the middle vehicle, carrying crushed limestone as a load. All are in the plain freight brown livery and are in POOL 5017 train. (Author's Ref No W8544/DL)

13T ROD IN COIL (COIL S) (KSV) Wagons

These vehicles were former 13T Highfits of the wooden bodied variety with cut-down ends, new sides and floor modifications to carry wire rod in coils in a single lateral stack along the middle of the wagon. In transit the load was normally sheeted. Suitable stock from various sources was used and numbers were as follows:

B477062/74/7, B477100/11/9/28/36/73/5/81/90/1/6, B477217/22/8/33/4/76/9/86/95, B477313/7/47/52 /63/6/84, B477411/20/51/94/7, B477500/4/11/25/7/31/44/50/92/4, B477637/47/8, B483759/72/6/84, B483807/49/72/82/90, B438907/13/38/43/52/65/7/70/4/8, B495158/63, B495210/3/43/56/67.

E275094, E275235/59/64, E275359, E275454/91, E275566/74, E275678, E275834/57, E275988, E276018/25/33/60, E276115, E276203/14/44/60/95, E276336/51/8/86/8, E276443/94, E276515/47/54/6 /62/81, E276637/40/4/50/4/72/93, E276703/21, E276802/40, E276940/1/72, E277031/45, E277112, E277221/44, E277311/20/41/61/7/93, E277418/43, E310993, E311002/12/22/37/42/7/56/64/76/91, E311118/27, E311203/44, E311364, E311454/97, E311501/8/16/36/93/6, E311658/81/7, E311716/24/50 /84/7, E311800/13/32/47/58/71, E311913/31/7, E312031, E312101/19/24/57/92, E312231/43/94, E312306/34/7/46/9/60/70/4/82, E312411/43/63/90/5/6/9, E312524/59/72/3/9, E312608/13/34/44, E312728/56/83/7, E312809/20/44/8/9/57/62/74/94, E312954/79/84/91, E313011/46/59, E313104/18.

M415369, M415780, M415858/70/7, M415909/16/49/52, M416037/93, M416249/71, M416321/46/83, M416526, M416670/4/96, M416724/65/73/95, M416912/76, M417131/62/82, M417250, M417407/63 /95, M417505/20/2/31/7, M417841/72/8/97, M417962/70/90, M418005, M418106/64/6/8, M418282, M418325/7, M418517/20, M418604/63/89/92, M418862/91/5, M418937/62, M419022, M419120, M419211/57, M419311/35/6, M419420/6/37/56/61/4/88/97, M419512/25/32.

S11879, S11900/3/6/25/35/89, S12035/51/68/75/96, S12187, S12267/87, S12310/32/4/76, S12416/52/ 61/2, S12504/29/33/43/65/86, S12621/67/82, S12714/48/55/63, S12840/5/94, S12919/25/45/77/9/84, S13002/7/83, S13148/80, S13260, S13319/80, S13424/37, S13515/37/66/8/89, S13603/32/92/5, S13743/5, S13815/45/51/75, S13911/23, S14030, S38364/76, S38401/14/8, S38539/47/91, S38647/9/99, S38704/42.

W148029/34, W148142/55/77/84, W148255/62, W148317/87/9, W148451/63, W148528/76, W148653/5, W148700/15/8/61, W148814/48.

Conversion was carried out circa 1971 and 426 wagons were converted. Initially, they were used between Scunthorpe and other steel works but they regularly served other destinations as well in later years. The original code was COIL S and this was changed to KSV under the TOPS system. All had been scrapped by the end of the review period for this volume.

E277246 taken at Scunthorpe, Lincolnshire in February 1978. This COIL S was converted from a former LNER vacuum-braked wagon by BR circa 1956. Still carrying the pre–TOPS code, it is sheeted with blue translucent plastic sheet, the normal for this load under transit. (Author's Ref No W7387/ DL)

B477276 taken at Battersea, South East London in November 1977. This was an unfitted High wagon originally, which was vacuum-braked circa 1959, hence the OLEO hydraulic buffers. Once the larger KRV wagons became available, the two types regularly worked together as seen here. (Author's Ref No W7014/DL)

W148034 taken at Rochester, Kent in April 1974. Only 22 former GWR wagons were converted to COIL S configuration. This location regularly received such loads from Scunthorpe in a variety of wagons. Tare weight: 6-6. (Author's Ref No W4551/DL)

S12840 taken at Wrexham, North Wales in April 1977. This former SR wagon was an unfitted High vacuum-braked by BR circa 1957. The KSV code was seen as early as 1977 but seems to have been rarely applied. (Author's Ref No W6450/DL)

22T ROD IN COIL (COIL R) (KRV) Wagons

This conversion was based on 22T Plate VB wagons and served the same steel works at Scunthorpe as the COIL S/KSV class. All plate bodywork was removed and wooden frames replaced this. The higher capacity allowed two rows of coil to be loaded and the floor modifications reflected this. All source vehicles were the later batches of BR-built PLATE VB wagons and varied only in having HYBOX axleboxes and self-contained buffers or roller-bearing axleboxes and OLEO hydraulic buffers. Numbers were as follows:

B934028/9/32/41/52/9/65/70/9/85/7/90/4/5/8, B934109-11/9/39/49/52/3/5/9/66/7/79/84/7/90/1, B934203/4/14/6/8/9/23/4/9/49/53/4/7/65/78/80/2/7/90/1, B934304/8/21/30/1/7/48/58/65/6-71/81 /9/99, B934420/1/3/5/8/34-7/40/2/6-9/52/5/9/62/9/74/86/90/5, B934506/11/3/4/6/8/22/8-30/5/40 /9/57/8/62-4/6/71/6/93, B934602/8/20/4/8/31-3/7/9/42/5/8/9/52/4/9/62/4/76/86/96/8/9, B934702 /5/6/9/11/3-6/9/30/6/40/9/65/70/6/81/5/7/9/90, B934806/14/8/24/32/9/41/2/5/6/52/9/62/3/71/5/7 /80-3/91/4/5/9, B934901/7/15/20/1/5/7-9/35/6/40/50/3/71/82, B935002/5/32/44/59/68/70/7/8/88 /90/5, B935104/12/3/8/21-3/7/32/49/54/64/6/7/72/4-6/87/91-3, B935204/7/9/11/3/4/25/9-31/3/5 /41/4/52/5/63/9/72/9/84/5/8/9/94-7, B935300/1/7/19/26/7/9/37/9/41/2/7/51/3/78/81/8/92, B935401-3/7/24/6/7/34/50/71/5-7/83/7/9, B935501/3/4/8/13/21/4/8/34/9/51/62/71/6/82/96, B935603/4/8-10/4/21/4/31/6/7/42/4/55/8/66/72/5/6/9/82/93/4, B935701/5/11/2/23/6/30/2/7/54/6 /62-4/81/3/4/8/9, B935803/4/6/9/10/4/6/7/20/5/8/9/38/45/9/54/5/60/3/8/9/74/8/84/93-5, B935901/12/21/38/47/9/51/4-6/9/63/4/72/4/6/9-82/9/96, B936005/8/9/12/5/6/31/40/4/6-8/51/4/5 /61/2/5/9/73/5/7, B936102/4/12/5/9/33/4/7/8/57/9/70/1/9/86/8/90/2, B936205/7/9/10/3-5/26/36 /41/3/5/53/7/60/1/82/9/92/3, B936301/13/6/34/5/9/42/3/51/66/74-6/83, B936403/8/10/22/7/42/7 /54/61/7/9/71/3/81/8/96/8, B936505/7/19/23.

This conversion was carried out slightly later than the COIL S/KSV and was given a corrupted code of COIL Krv. The COIL was very quickly deleted leaving the correct KRV code, albeit in incorrect script. 498 wagons were converted and 423 remained in service at the end of the review period. The code was then changed to SRV but this will be dealt with in more detail in the next volume.

This line of wagons taken at Scunthorpe awaiting the next load shows the modifications of both KRV and KSV wagons. (Author's Ref No W2221/DL)

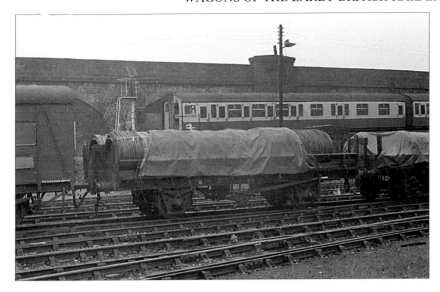

B934516 taken at Battersea, South East London in March 1980. This is one of the PLATE VB wagons built with self-contained buffers, but the HYBOX axleboxes have since been replaced with roller bearings. A KSV wagon is on the right and the KRV seems to have been given the sheet for the smaller type, as it does not fully cover the load. (Author's Ref No W8930/DL)

B935979 taken at Cardiff (Tidal Sidings) in November 1983. By the time this view was taken, it seems that Cardiff GKN works were doing the wire coil and this KRV is loaded and sheeted in a different manner. The vehicle on the right is a KEV wagon. (Author's Ref No W13609/DL)

B934216 taken at Rochester, Kent in February 1976. The COIL Krv code was usually painted on the side bar but, as this was frequently covered by the sheet, recoded vehicles had the code on the small original side. This conversion is one of the early type with self-contained buffers and HYBOX axleboxes. (Author's Ref No W5674/DL)

22T ROD IN COIL (KEV) Wagons

The KEV conversion was rather later than the previous two classes and was initiated in 1978. These vehicles operated from the Guest, Keen & Nettlefold works in Cardiff, South Wales. The conversion was not so involved. The original sides were retained and uprights welded inside the original ends; floor battens on the pattern of the KRV were fitted. The range of chassis variations was wider as the whole of BR's PLATE VB fleet were involved, including a few former LNER wagons. Numbers were as follows:

B931134/70/5, B931213, B931301/41/85, B931513, B931602/32/64, B931730/49/57, B931862, B932007/44, B932109/42/78, B932223, B932457/63/8/96, B932545, B932693, B932731, B932830/4/6/90, B932923/5/52, B933019/24/8/34/73/88/9/95, B933102/32/51/69/86/93, B933214/45/52/61/92/2, B933301/11/3/57, B933403/27/9/88, B933501/2730/84/5/97, B933603/24/30/71/83/5/99, B933720/6/43/5/53/4/67/80/8, B933859/70/7, B933928, B934003/18/24/5/40/5/97, B934118/40/74/89, B934207/10/44/74, B934357/73/8/96, B934403/61/3, B934544/5/7/85, B934610/38/41/78/89/97, B934834/7/8/84/5, B934918/45/70/93/7, B935004/96, B935102/15/59/94, B935227/34/54, B935333/55/77, B935408/10/33/58/69/81, B935512/25/48, B935602 /11/20/6/65/7, B935728/31/6/40/76/90, B935802/19/51/65/72/85, B935906/24/8/57, B936029/57/89, B936113/40/5, B935206/21/51/63/5, B936303/45/56/67/78, B936448/84, B936500, E292204/12/40, E292327. (Also possibly KEV were B933538, B934046, B935274, B935412, B935821).

E292204 taken at Hoo Junction, Rochester in November 1980. When unloaded and viewed from the side, this class of rod-in-coil wagon was hard to identify apart from the steel end stanchions. This example is a former LNER PLATE VB wagon and retains oil axleboxes and spindle buffers. (Author's Ref No W10001/DL)

B932142 taken at Warrington (Arpley) in February 1982. The loaded wagon seen in this shot is well sheeted, to the point of being dangerous at the nearer end of the vehicle. This example was formerly unfitted and vacuum-braked in 1958, when it received roller bearings and OLEO hydraulic buffers. (Author's Ref No W10238/DL)

B933193 taken at Cardiff (Tidal Sidings) in November 1983. Most KEV rod-in-coil wagons started their loaded journey at this location and this example is rather better sheeted. This was to the same basic design as E292204 on the previous page but was BR-built. It retains all original plate features. (Author's Ref No W13610/DL)

B934274 taken at Warrington (Arpley) in February 1982. The next vehicle to the one at the top of this page, here the sheet has become rumpled and the load exposed. It is entirely possible that both wagons were stopped to have the sheets properly fitted. The problem was that sheets for 17ft 6in long vehicles were being used and the tying of two together was not very successful. This example was of the PLATE VB with HYBOX axleboxes and self-contained buffers. (Author's Ref No W11270/DL)

Steel-carrying Wagons (Strip Coil Conversions) and other related wagons

To replace the converted Palbrick COIL P wagons featured in the previous volume, which had of course subsequently been converted to 16T Mineral wagons, Bogie Bolster E wagons were converted and coded BEV (probably technically semi-permanent conversions) or JPV. The conversions, probably carried out circa 1977, differed visually. Type 1 used two or three cradles from the Palbrick conversions and original bolsters. Type 2 used original bolsters placed longitudinally, which made the load higher. The JPV code was changed to BWV in 1983 but was probably never carried on the wagons as all were withdrawn by 1984. Numbers were as follows:
Type 1 (BEV)
B923372/85, B923450/94, B923513/66, B923618/92, B923715, B923883, B923938/92, B924024, B924129/53, B924257/86, B924334/89, B924820/48/53/8/73.
Type 2 (JPV)
B923386, B923421/45, B923635, B923758, B923906, B924049, B924253, B924318/60.
Type Unrecorded
B923345/67, B923420/47/55/83, B923526/9/54/6, B923602/6/7/13/42/68/89/90, B923714/34/78, B923824/44/54/9/78/90/5/6, B923909/17/28/56/68/76/91, B924042/75, B924107/9/27/49/51, B924220/44/9/65/83/4, B924323/53/9, B924813/21/36.

Another Bogie Bolster E conversion was carried out in 1971 and provided standard longitudinal coil cradles, with hoods. Coded R COIL VB, then JRV, most became S&T department cable laying wagons in due course. Numbers were as follows:

B923480, B923548, B923617/86, B923732/70/80, B923805/9/14/98, B924020/85, B924108/36, B924207, B924338/47/73/82.

Other Bogie Bolster E conversions that cannot be illustrated were COIL RR (B923495, converted 1974) and BOGIE HOT-COIL U (B923346/9/95/8, B923419, B923537, B923614/45, B923717, B923836/65/91, B923904/39, B924003/13/30, B924111, B924341, B924855, converted 1972).

B960000 to B960023 were numbers issued to a motley group of former BORAIL WE wagons that carried strip coil over the bogies. Converted between 1974 and 1976, they were coded JXO and were withdrawn by the early 1980s.

A dual-purpose conversion, for vehicle or strip coil traffic, was the 1978 conversion of BOPLATE E VB wagons to FWV. The original sides were removed and numbers were as follows:

B947863-7/9/70/2-5/7/8/81/2/4-6/8/9/92/4/5/7-9, B947900-4/7-9/11/4/5/8/22/4-7/9/31/2/4/5/8-42/4/5/7-9 /51/3-7/9/61/-3/5/7/8/71/2/4/6/8-82/4/6-91/4-7/9, B948004/6/8/9.

Finally, a number of Iron Ore Tippler wagons were converted to carry ingot moulds, which are large metal castings. Holes were cut in the sides and the code SMO was allocated. Known examples were as follows:

B380150, B380393, B380410/85, B380582/97, B380634/61, B380708, B380859, B380937, B381069/90, B381123, B381230/43/82, B381300/47, B381426/94, B381583, B381628, B381853, B382109, B382263/8, B382316/66, B382498, B382524/38, B382654, B382728, B382806/70/96, B382965, B383027/53, B383101/35/74/7/87, B383403/31/2/41/59/67, B383605/55/68, B383738/96/7, B383888, B383907, B384017/36/97, B384118/55/66, B384257, B384300, B384405/19, B384510/9/96, B384618, B384702/5/39/81, B384843, B385029/93, B385130/82, B385258, B385307, B385599, B385628/30/8, B385756, B386257/88, B386425/42, B386641, B386837, B386940/53, B387021/33/42/8/96, B387102/17/33/46, B387205/58/79, B387379, B387404, B387530/44/88, B387657/74/82, B387749/75, B387887, B387970/7, B388032/57/84, B388106/14, B388356/68/71, B388401/9/33/5/45, B388518, B388660, B388754, B388813/28/73/5, B388930/42/45/8, B389026/67, B747647.

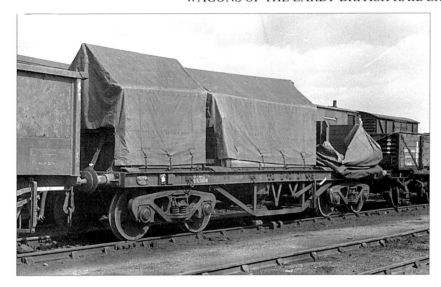

B923898 taken at Severn Tunnel Junction in October 1976. The R COIL VB seen here has a collapsed tarpaulin and is probably stopped for repairs. Before conversion to cable wagons, these wagons did operate without tarpaulins. (Author's Ref No W5610/DL)

B960000 taken at Bescot Yard, Walsall in November 1976. The first JXO, converted from B946000, is seen here recently out of Simonside wagon works and with a typical load, although only one coil is sheeted. (Author's Ref No W5860/DL)

B387042 taken at Warrington (Arpley) in April 1977. Not all the ingot mould wagons had side cut-outs. Some worked to South Wales, and received them, whilst the majority operated to Workington, as seen here. The lettering is black on yellow. (Author's Ref No W6230/DL)

Bogie Pipe-carrying Wagons

The standard 12 ton capacity 12ft 0in wheelbase Pipe wagon had been developed for main drainage schemes using a standard length of drain pipe manufactured at Stanton & Staveley Ltd works in the Erewash valley near Toton marshalling yard. In the early 1970s, there was a need for longer vehicles to convey much larger pipes built at locations such as Corby and Hartlepool. These were moved by rail to Leith Docks, Scotland, coated and shipped out to North Sea Gas fields.

The first conversion involved vacuum-braked Bogie Plate wagons and the sides were removed and wooden supports for five pipes, fixed over the bogies, provided on the floor. This was carried out before 1974 and was improperly recorded. Known examples are as follows:
B947863, B948145, B948207 and B948219.

Somewhat similar was a 1974 conversion of vacuum-braked Bogie Bolster C wagons, and the Bogie Bolster H derivative. With these wagons, which were coded BTV, the supports were for three pipes of greater diameter; the supports were positioned inboard of the bogies and blue straps were used to secure the pipes. Numbers for these are as below:
B922527/30/54/8, B922650, B922704/20/60/85, B922860/77, B922943, B923021/48/96, B924461, B924538/94, B924616, B945795, B945866/77/80.

Additional wagons were converted in 1982 and two sizes of pipe could be carried. Numbers were as follows:

37ft outside diameter pipes (BT 001A)
B922520/1/42/53/70/89/99, B922615/7/24/5/7/32/45/9/54/78/86, B922702/38/50/9/76/80/90, B922809 /12/24/56/7/77/9/81/7/93/8, B922910/44/58/89/97, B923000/1/7/35/8/40/2/52/4, B923100/22/36/9/40/9 /52/62/75/87, B923204/5/42/4/6/8/9/54/74, B924402/21/44/54/5/63/4/9/70/81/7, B924512/20/37/44/50/3 /7/70/89, B924606/12/44/64/84/97, B924706/10/42/4/60/4/9/78/92, B945851/71, B945976.
42ft outside diameter pipes (BT 002A)
B922530/46/55/60/71, B922605/35/65/6, B911716/69/77, B922807/14/26/82/5, B922911/2/24/86/90, B923010/3/30/1/43/5/79/83/8, B923105/20/38/57/68/78, B923219/56/63/79/98, B924419/30/75/7, B924502/8/33/56/65/90, B924600/1/39/40, B924713/76/85, B945794/5/7, B945800/37/44/54/65/88, B945927/30/1/2/62/7/77/80/3.

Another early variant, coded Bogie Bolster Q and given diagram 1/479 (suggesting a pre-1972 date for this conversion) had no bolsters or straps, the load being held by tall stanchions. Numbers for these were as follows:
B922502/33/5/8/66/8, B922633/9/55/83, B922715/9/68/74/83/8, B922827/52/69, B922903/21/6/42/50/6 /75/87, B923004/20/33/6/77/92/8, B923173/86/90, B923233/59/89/97, B924410/27/45/59/74/90/1, B924516/23/54/71/5, B924622/9/34/51, B924770/80/6, B945822/43/7/73/85, B945903/12/40/4/6/70.

These, with certain exceptions (B922715, B945822/43/7/73/85, B945903/12/40/4/6/70), received curved floor supports and new curved stanchions in 1981. Further vehicles were added, as below:
B922556, B922746/63, B922810, B923158, B923210/4/45, B924404/27/61, B924519/36/60/6/99, B924711/99.

In truth, this fleet appears to have undergone constant change and photographs should be used to ascertain configuration at a given date. Survivors received air through-pipes in later years.

A final conversion, converted circa 1974 and broken up circa 1982, was the BOV class. It was designed for tubes of narrow diameter loaded in two blocks between tall wooden frames and held in by massive stanchions. Numbers were as follows:
B924429/34/53/65/6/79/80/8/95/9, B924504/7/9/18/24/5/9/32/59/67/77/9/92/3/6, B924602/3/11/25 /31/5/6/41/5/55/66-8/78/86/91/2, B924705/35/58/9/62/6/73/87-9/92.

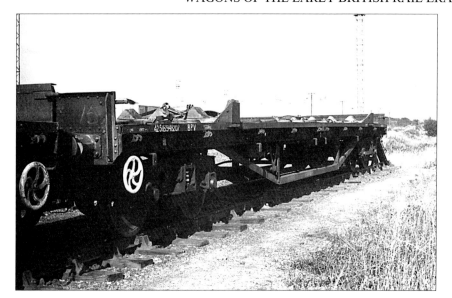

B948207 taken at Severn Tunnel Junction in November 1975. These early BOPLATE E VB conversions may not have been specifically for the North Sea gas pipe traffic, as none of the few examples recorded by me were found where such traffic could be expected. (Author's Ref No W5710/DL)

B924461 taken at Stanton Gate, Derbyshire in April 1976. This vehicle was operating as a Bogie Bolster H when converted, and retains the code for that class and also the yellow vertical stripes associated with it. (Author's Ref No W5411/DL)

B923080 taken at Teesport Docks in April 1983. This was another Bogie Bolster H with the new BQV code but retaining the yellow stripes. The narrow stanchions do not look particularly sturdy. This particular wagon does not feature in any of the recorded lists, illustrating the problems with identifying all these North Sea gas pipe wagons. (Author's Ref No W13008/DL)

Barrier Wagons (RBV, RBX, etc)

Barrier wagons had always been part of the wagon fleet, generally placed between locomotives, brake vans and rolling stock, usually tank wagons containing inflammable loads, but it was only after 1972 that they became formerly recognised as such and were coded RBV or RBX, depending on the brake gear. As far as is known, there were no unfitted RBO wagons. Various types were used and details of some known examples are as follows:

Cattle Wagons (used on sand trains from Oakamoor to Stoke-on-Trent to prevent sand blowing into brake vans)
TDB892057, TDB892280, B893350, TDB893448, B894204.
Ferry Vans (used with air-braked railtanks for spirits and dangerous chemicals)
B786884, B786892, B786921, B786926, B786959, B786967, B786969, B786993, B786996, B786998, B787005, B787101, B787117, B787180, B787186, B787260, B787275, B787318, B787332.
Long-wheelbase Pallet Vans (FORD vans) (used with air-braked railtanks for spirits and dangerous chemicals)
B787067.
Ferry CCT Car-carrying Vans (used with air-braked railtanks for spirits and dangerous chemicals)
B889009, B889014, B889022.
Insulated Fish Vans (ex passenger) (used with vacuum-braked railtanks for spirits and dangerous chemicals)
E87620, E87720, E87820, E87857, E87908, M87664, M87832, W87573, W87715, W87773, W87985.
Ale Pallet Wagons (usually with sides removed) (used with vacuum-braked railtanks for spirits and dangerous chemicals)
B730620, B730794, B732072, B732589, B732693, B732868, B732922.
Plate Wagons (unfitted to air-piped circa 1968) (used with air-braked railtanks for spirits and dangerous chemicals) (coded REACH wagons)
TDB931631, TDB931716, B931747, B931873, TDB931937, B932919.
Ferry CAR C Car-carrying Wagons (used with air-braked railtanks for spirits and dangerous chemicals) (coded REACH wagons)
TDB748132, B748136, TDB748143.

All the above can be confirmed photographically. There were probably other individuals but no other classes involved.

B786921 taken at Millerhill Yard in November 1982. This van still carries the original bauxite livery with only the BR double arrow symbol but many examples carried the later rail grey/flame red livery introduced in the late 1970s. (Author's Ref No W12336/DL)

B889009 taken at Spondon, Derbyshire in May 1982. Former ferry vehicles were favoured as barrier wagons because they had air-brakes, as did the stock they worked with. The bogie railtank seen here, however, was probably vacuum-braked. (Author's Ref No W11533/DL)

B732589 taken at Ellesmere Port, Wirral in February 1982. This was the third incarnation of this vehicle; firstly TUBE VB, then ALE PALLET. Not long afterwards, it was to be scrapped. (Author's Ref No W10533/DL)

B748132 taken at Hoo Junction, Rochester in November 1975. In the 1970s, the plate and former CAR C wagons were considered departmental stock. Livery was olive green and a TD (for Traffic) prefix added to the number. (Author's Ref No W5353/DL)

Runner Wagons (RRO, RRV)

In a similar manner to barrier wagons, runner wagons had always been available but they had always been, perforce, low-height wagons. Under the TOPS system, this became more formalised. Unfitted stock was used, as RRO, and braked stock were RRB, RRV and RRX. Pure air-braked stock, converted from vehicles in the next section of this book, had begun to appear by the end of the review period, but these will be covered in full in the next volume.

Ferry CAR C Car-carrying Wagons (unmodified, coded RRX)
B748134.
Ferry Vans (bodywork removed, coded RRX)
B787108, B787116, B787188, B787324.
Long-wheelbase Pallet Vans (FORD vans) (bodywork removed, coded RRB)
B787400/3/26/31/5/60/74
Timber Wagons (ends cut and folded into body, coded RRV)
B455503/14/9/22/4/7/36/8/45/7.
Unfitted Plate Wagons (bodywork removed, coded FLAT, then RRO)
B920324, B930156, B930976, B931148, B931205, E202371, E242262, E242360, E286429, M726077, M726339.
Vacuum-braked Plate Wagons (sides and ends folded into body, coded RRV)
B931831/41, B931934, B932081, B932657/90, B932770, B932823/70, B932960/8/79/97, B933065, B933192, B933334, B933434/41, B933543/75, B933612/39, B933716/30/6/58, B933864/5/92, B933931/67/75, B934019, B934100/95, B934215/89, B934460, B934536/41, B934601, B934769/79, B934989, B935037, B935365/85, B935541/59, B935755, B935821, B935962, B936444/57, E292180, E292215/7, E292304/43.
Conflat conversions (coded RRV)
B733091, B932887, B933451, B933846, B935915/33.
Lowmac Wagons (not converted usually, unless CONFLAT ISO)
B904106/9/17/38, B904511, B904711.

As with the barrier wagons, all the above vehicles were photographed and there was great variety. The RRO wagons were fairly early conversions and were withdrawn, to be replaced by the RRV fleet. The RRB and RRX class were later conversions and probably replaced the bulk of the RRV fleet from 1982 onwards.

B733091 taken at Scunthorpe, Lincolnshire in February 1978. This wagon was illustrated in Volume 3 of this series (page 19). Here it is seen after the Speedfreight experiment ceased, in unmodified state now in use as a runner wagon. The adjacent bogie bolster looks to be unfitted, negating the vacuum brakegear of the runner. (Author's Ref No W7322/DL)

B455519 taken at Tring, Hertfordshire in September 1982. At first glance, not a particularly suitable wagon for conversion to a runner, which involved cutting the ends, the relatively young age of this class was probably the deciding factor. (Author's Ref No W11967/DL)

787418 taken at Hoo Junction, Rochester in December 1988. Once the van bodywork had been removed, the weight of these conversions was insufficient for higher speed trains. Scrap rail was therefore fixed longitudinally to the floor. (Author's Ref No W14388/DL)

B931205 taken at York Station Yard in November 1977. The original unfitted ex-Plate conversions were never expected to travel at great speed and therefore had no extra weight. The FLAT code was probably applied by the NER, which was familiar with such vehicles, but the wagon was not intended as a load carrier. (Author's Ref No W6939/DL)

Air-braked Open Wagons (OPEN AB/OAA)

Numerically the first air-braked fleet wagons were the open wagons and the OPEN AB (later OAA) was the first of this group.

Built on the standard 20ft 9in chassis, the original springs were always retained. Three-part six-plank wooden drop sides were fitted and the solid steel ends matched the sides in height. The brakegear rigging and brake levers were of the earliest pattern. They were painted freight brown with white double arrow symbol and black on yellow ABN disc; as far as is known, none ever received maroon livery. Rail grey/flame red variants and black/yellow "sector" did appear, however, and will be covered in the next volume. Building and numbering details were as follows:

100000 to 100099   45T OPEN (diagram 1/191)   10/1971 to 12/1971   3727   BR (Ashford)

A further 50 vehicles (to have been numbered 100100 to 100149) were cancelled.

100043 was converted to the prototype OBA in 1974 and will be covered in the next section of this volume. Certain vehicles, such as 100022, 100027, 100048 and 100077, were given end extensions, as for the OBA class but not quite so tall, and were allocated to REDLAND traffic, the vehicles carrying a pale green bodywork with REDLAND plates. It is not known exactly when this conversion was done, or how many vehicles, but they probably operated from the Peterborough area.

By 1991, almost all the fleet were in civil engineers use, as ZDA SQUID wagons, although some were transferred back to revenue traffic; this included the REDLAND wagons. 100060 had been withdrawn; 100034/42/84/6 were listed as to a different design code (OA 001B, as opposed to the standard OA 001A); these could have been the REDLAND conversions but my records do not prove this.

100012 taken at Nunhead, South East London in May 1977. Marshalled in a train of similar wagons, this example is still coded OPEN AB and retains some vestiges of the original symbols. (Author's Ref No W7539/DL)

100008 taken at Battersea, South West London in April 1980. The OPEN AB class were provided with purpose-built grey plastic sheets, as shown in the vehicle on the left. This wagon is covered by a blue transparent plastic sheet covering a load of newsprint rolls. (Author's Ref No W8997/ DL)

100029 taken at Southampton in November 1979. This wagon has been recoded OAA but retains the original livery and symbols. The painted name CORPACH suggest newsprint rolls as a regular load but it is here seen loaded with empty cable drums. (Author's Ref No W9032/DL)

DC100022 taken at Hither Green, South East London in April 1992. Although seen after transfer to the civil engineers and coded SQUID, this is one of the REDLAND conversions still in the pale green livery Note the cut-outs in the lower sides for blue nylon straps. (Author's Ref No W16813/DL)

Air-braked Open Wagons (OBA)

The prototype OBA, 110000 (initially allocated 450000 because it resembled a steel-carrying wagon of the Tube class) which was converted from OPEN AB number 100043, was built in 1974. This carried a modified body, with four-part five-plank dropsides, extendable stanchions between door sections and raised ends. The latter were merely extension pieces grafted on to the original ends. Livery was maroon with the new combined Railfreight and double arrow symbol on the right-hand side.

This was followed by a production batch of five hundred wagons. The bodywork was as the prototype but with one-piece ends. Updated brakegear was used but the springs and suspension were the same as used on the OPEN AB class.

A second production batch followed, which was identical in every way except that German Brunninghaus springs and suspension were fitted.

Livery for both batches when new was as the prototype, although many were later repainted in rail grey / flame red livery and at least one in black/yellow "Sector" livery. By 1981, vehicles from the first batch were receiving Brunninghaus springs and suspension but there were no other significant conversions during the period covered by this volume. Numbers and building details were as follows:

110000	45T OPEN (OB 001A)	1974	3861 BR (Shildon)
110001 to 110500	45T OPEN (OB 001B)	10/1977 to 4/1979	3909 BR (Ashford)
110501 to 110800	45T OPEN (OB 001C)	12/1978 to 9/1979	3930 BR (Shildon)

110000 taken at New Cross Gate, South East London in September 1982. Although seen in civil engineers use, the OBA prototype has here retained the original livery and demonstrates the end extensions to advantage in this view. (Author's Ref No W11918A/DL)

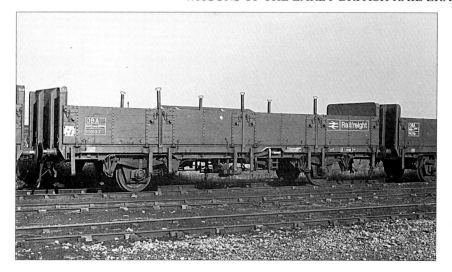

110137 taken at Scunthorpe, Lincolnshire in November 1980. This view of the lot 3909 production batch shows the clean lines of the OBA class and has the side stanchions raised. This feature was presumably to support wagon sheets. (Author's Ref No W9044/DL)

110258 taken at Hoo Junction in August 1982. Members of the OBA class were true general merchandise wagons and could carry a variety of loads. Here the load is maritime buoys of a khaki colour, probably for military use. (Author's Ref No W11603/DL)

110674 taken at Battersea, South West London in August 1980. The OBA class was well suited to wire coil traffic and, although there were other types available, a train loaded with this commodity is seen here. (Author's Ref No W9056/DL)

Air-braked Vans (Early Batches, VAB/VBB/VBA)

In contrast to the open wagon designs, the early van fleet was very complicated.

200000 to 200208   45T VAN (diagram 1/248)   6/1969 to 12/1970   3685   BR (Ashford)

These were the first air-braked stock, other than MGR hoppers and Freightliners to appear. Coded COV AB, they were painted freight brown with double arrow symbol and black on yellow ABN disc. All were air-braked and vacuum through-piped and had the early pattern brakegear and springs and suspension. These vans were originally allocated B787480 to B787698. It was realised subsequently that a batch of twenty vehicles, 200100 to 200119, had been given end ventilators and these were given the TOPS code VAB. The remainder (200000 to 200099 and 200120 to 200208) were to become VBB. Unfortunately, some depots merely painted out the first two letters of the COV AB code, leaving an incorrect VAB on vans without ventilators.

200210 to 200219   45T VAN (various diagrams)   7/1970 to 11/1970   3727   BR (Ashford)

This group of vans all had the same bodywork but had different experimental suspension systems. Bodywork was as the first batch, without end ventilators; the suspension was referred to as Director of Design Mk III on 200210 to 200214 (diagram 1/259) and Director of Design Mk II on 200215 to 200219 (diagram 1/258). All were air-braked and vacuum through-piped. The TOPS code was VBB.

200220 TO 200228   45T VAN (diagram 1/253)   10/1970 to 11/1970   3686 BR (Ashford)

This group of vans were the same as lot 3727, except that all had Taperlite experimental suspension. These vans were originally allocated B787710 to B787719. The TOPS code was VBB.

200230 to 200239   45T VAN (diagram 1/254)   10/1969 to 3/1970   3687 BR (Ashford)

This group of vans were the same as lot 3727, except that all had Director Design Mk I experimental suspension. These vans were originally allocated B787720 to B787729. The TOPS code was VBB.

200240 to 200249   45T VAN (diagram 1/257)   9/1969 to 11/1969   3696 BR (Shildon)

This group of vans were the same as lot 3727, except that all had BR long-link experimental suspension. These vans were originally allocated B787700 to B787709. The TOPS code was VBB.

200250 to 200324   45T VAN (diagram 1/257)   11/1970 to 8/1971   3726 BR (Ashford)
200550 to 200649   45T VAN   12/1974 to 4/1975   3840 BR (Shildon)

These vans were the production version of lot 3696 and kept the same diagram number. The only difference was that they were air-braked only from 200300. The first batch was coded COV AB and later VBB or VBA. As they did not have vents, the second batch was originally incorrectly coded VAA. This was eventually changed to the correct VBA.

The situation became more confused when the vacuum through-pipes were removed from those vans so fitted. All vans, except 200550 to 200649, were delivered in freight brown. The exceptions were in maroon livery and significant numbers of the others received this livery as well. The small number that received rail grey / flame red and black/yellow "sector" liveries will be covered in the next volume. Apart from withdrawals and transfer to departmental sections, none seem to have been converted for other duties.

200093 taken at Barry, South Wales in November 1971. This early view of a diagram 1/248 van shows evidence of a Kelloggs poster. Full original freight brown livery is carried with COV AB code but no ABN disc. Tare weight: 10-7. (Author's Ref No W3982/DL)

200017 taken at Fratton Yard, Portsmouth in April 1980. This diagram 1/248 van has been repainted in full maroon livery with appropriate symbols and VBB code. At this stage the vacuum through-pipe was retained. (Author's Ref No: W3964/DL)

200117 taken at Battersea, SW London in April 1976. One of the 20 un-diagrammed ventilated vans, this example has received full maroon livery and appropriate symbols, including correct VAB code, the vacuum through-pipe being still fitted. (Author's Ref No W6581/BR)

200216 taken at Birkenhead Docks in November 1978. All the vans in this section had full-length doors, which can be seen partially open in this view. Livery is freight brown with double arrow symbol, very faded ABN disc and VBB code. This is one of the diagram 1/258 experimental suspension batch. (Author's Ref No W4638/DL)

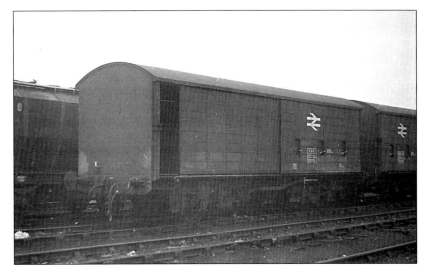

200227 taken at Fratton Yard, Portsmouth in April 1980. This is a diagram 1/253 experimental suspension vehicle in freight brown livery with double arrow symbol but no ABN disc. Code is COV AB but the tare weight is metric. (Author's Ref No W4974/DL)

200232 taken at Llandeilo Junction, South Wales in August 1981. This diagram 1/254 experimental suspension van has an interesting livery mixture. Main body colour is freight brown with ABN disc and VBB code, with the Railfreight legend and symbols on a maroon rectangle. (Author's Ref No W8998/DL)

200247 taken at Birkenhead Docks in February 1979. This is a diagram 1/257 experimental suspension van retaining full freight brown livery with double arrow symbol, ABN disc and COV AB code. Only the metric tare weight is new. (Author's Ref No W5135/DL)

200266 taken at Nunhead, South East London in April 1977. This is a lot 3726 van in original condition with freight brown livery, double arrow symbol, ABN disc and COV AB code, albeit with metric tare weight. (Author's Ref No W6814/DL)

200587 taken at Nunhead, SE London in April 1977. Marshalled between two lot 3856 VDA vans, this shows the lot 3840 VBA van in maroon livery with Railfreight symbol and the incorrect VAA code initially applied. (Author's Ref No W6812/DL)

Air-braked Vans (Centre door, VCA/VCB)

The final van from the first batch was built with centre-opening doors and introduced a new design, although the production batch had more door handles. This prototype was transferred to the CM&EE in later years and building details are below.

200209   45T VAN (diagram 1/265)   1/1972   3739 BR (Ashford)

Two production batches were built with BR long-link suspension and air-brakes only. The first batch was delivered in freight brown livery with double arrow symbol and COV CD code. The ABN disc does not appear to have been applied. One (200386) was recorded coded INSULATED BANANA VAN, without any symbols, but little is known about this variant. The second batch was also delivered in freight brown livery with double arrow symbol. An incorrect VBA code was applied because of the problems referred to in the previous section. Building details are as follows:

200325 to 200449   45T VAN (diagram 1/262)   8/1971 to 2/1972   3764 BR (Ashford)
200450 to 200549   45T VAN   7/1974 to 11/1974   3832 BR (Shildon)

Maroon livery was applied to the first batch in due course, as was rail grey/flame red. None received black/yellow "sector" livery as a high proportion of the vans were transferred to the departmental fleets. There were some conversions, to container flats and runners, and these will be covered in the next volume.

ADC200209 taken at Severn Tunnel Junction in November 1983. Now coded ZRB, this prototype centre-door van is in maroon livery with Railfreight symbols. It was vacuum-piped from new and would have been coded VCB. (Author's Ref No W13409/DL)

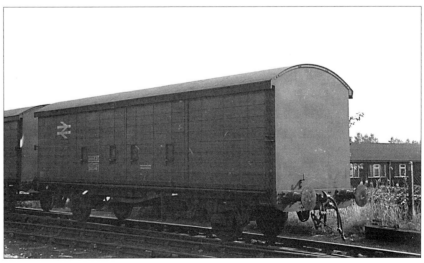

200365 taken at Manchester (Trafford Park) in August 1973. In freight brown livery with double arrow symbol and COV CD code, but no ABN disc and a metric tare weight, this van represents the original VCA. (Author's Ref No W4421/DL)

200389 taken at York Dringhouses Yard in February 1979. This lot 3764 van has been fully repainted in maroon livery with Railfreight symbol and VCA code. As it is not coupled to the vehicles on either side, this wagon mixture would be unlikely away from a marshalling yard. (Author's Ref No W6507/DL)

200456 taken at Briton Ferry, South Wales in November 1975. This lot 3832 van is in original condition in freight brown livery with double arrow symbol, no ABN disc and incorrect VBA code. It is marshalled into a block train of similar vans. (Author's Ref No W6288/DL)

200476 taken at Warrington (Arpley) in February 1982. None of the lot 3832 vans appear to have been painted in maroon livery and went straight to rail grey / flame red, as seen with this example. The correct VCA code was applied at this time. (Author's Ref No W10585/DL)

Air-braked Vans (VDA)

After various door experiments, the VDA class was produced as the standard van design for the mid-1970s. The door release catches were spaced out and the doors opened centrally. Brakegear and suspension was BR long-link design but two batches had modifications. Lot 3890 vans had brake shoes rather than disc brakes and lot 3856 had Taperlite suspension. Livery for all was maroon with standard symbols when new. Lot 3890 vans had white roofs, indicating, it is believed, allocation to Rowntree's chocolate traffic and one was erroneously painted all-white. Batch details are as below:

200650 to 200979	45T VAN (VD 001A)	1/1976 to 11/1976	3855	BR (Ashford)
200980 to 200999	45T VAN (VD 001B)	9/1976 to 11/1976	3890	BR (Ashford)
201000 to 201099	45T VAN (VD 001C)	11/1975 to 3/1976	3856	BR (Shildon)
210100 to 210399	45T VAN (VD 001A)	8/1977 to 11/1978	3908	BR (Shildon)

(Note: The numbers 201100 to 210099 were not issued due to an error at the BR office that had responsibility for issuing such numbers.)

There were significant numbers of conversions within this group. Those remaining as vans received rail grey/ flame red and black/yellow "sector" livery and all these will be covered in the next volume.

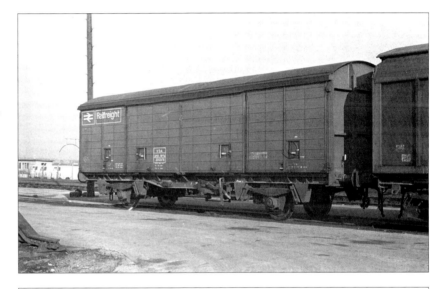

200976 taken at Worksop, Nottinghamshire in November 1980. The standard VDA van in original condition is represented by this lot 3855 vehicle. The ends, which had been plain on earlier designs, were now ribbed although it is not known what advantage this was. (Author's Ref No W9017/DL)

210214 taken at Barking, East London in April 1980. The vehicles of lot 3908 were built at Shildon Works rather than Ashford but there are no obvious differences. (Author's Ref No W7509/DL)

201081 taken at Dagenham, Essex in May 1982. The lot 3856 vans, with Taperlite suspension, were very obviously different from the standard VDA. This example is lettered CRAWLEY – HATFIELD – TRAFFORD PARK and may indicate a monitored circuit working to assess the experimental suspension. (Author's Ref No W11480/DL)

200999 taken at Dover, Kent in April 1981. The lot 3890 vans, with brake shoes, were not so easily spotted, and the white roof was the give-away. This may have aided heat dissipation to stop the load of chocolate from melting. The presence of three such vans at Dover may have indicated export traffic. (Author's Ref No W9019/DL)

200987 taken at York, Dringhouses Yard in April 1979. As far as is known, this was the only all-white van and, as the solebar is also white, it is assumed to have been a mistake by the painter not thought worth correcting. This van was probably withdrawn without repainting. (Author's Ref No W6886/DL)

Air-braked Covered Hopper Wagons (COVHOP AB/CBA)

This design was a covered variant of the merry-go-round coal hopper wagon specifically for lime traffic from Derbyshire. Apart from the new roof, all other details were as the HOP AB. The body panels were unpainted with freight brown framing and the solebar was black. Lettering and code were in black. The original code is thought to be COVHOP AB, although no code can be seen in any early photographs; the code CBA was applied after the introduction of TOPS. Due to the loss of some of the fleet in a serious accident, five identical vehicles were built to lot 3922. None featured in conversions and 35 were in service in 1991. Building details were as follows:

250000 to 250051	31T COVHOP (diagram 1/252)	5/1969 to 7/1969	3680	BR (Shildon)
250052 to 250056	31T COVHOP (CB 001A)	10/1977 to 11/1977	3922	BR (Shildon)

(Note: The lot 3680 wagons were originally allocated B870880 to B870931.)

250010 taken at Peak Forest, Derbyshire in May 1975. Due to the nature of the load, these wagons were always very dirty, making it hard to read the number/code panel. Note both hand brake levers pinned down in this hilly area. (Author's Ref No W4987/DL)

250046 taken at Burton-upon-Trent in September 1982. A repair depot for MGR hoppers was established at this location and this was also where the CBA fleet went for regular maintenance. The CBA code can just about be made out under the grime. (Author's Ref No W11881/DL)

Air-braked MGR Hopper Wagons (HAA)

Further batches of standard HAA merry-go-round hoppers were produced up until the end of the review period and details were as follows:

355797 to 356246	HAA Hopper (diagram 1/156)	8/1970 to 7/1971	3720 BR (Shildon)
356247 to 356746	HAA Hopper (diagram 1/156)	3/1971 to 2/1972	3751 BR (Shildon)
356747 to 357246	HAA Hopper (diagram 1/156)	3/1972 to 11/1972	3788 BR (Shildon)
357247 to 357396	HAA Hopper (HA 001A)	12/1973 to 6/1974	3815 BR (Shildon)
357397 to 358246	HAA Hopper (HA 002F)	6/1974 to 8/1975	3844 BR (Shildon)
358247 to 358496	HAA Hopper (HA 002F)	7/1975 to 11/1975	3864 BR (Shildon)
358497 to 358856	HAA Hopper (HA 002F)	11/1975 to 4/1976	3869 BR (Shildon)
358857 to 359176	HAA Hopper (HA 002F)	4/1976 to 10/1976	3882 BR (Shildon)
359177 to 359571	HAA Hopper (HA 002F)	8/1976 to 9/1977	3887 BR (Shildon)
365000 to 365299	HAA Hopper (HA 002C)	9/1980 to 11/1980	3978 BR (Shildon)
365300 to 365499	HAA Hopper (HA 002C)	11/1980 to 5/1981	3984 BR (Shildon)
365500 to 366129	HAA Hopper (HA 002C)	1/1981 to 1/1982	3997 BR (Shildon)

Certain wagons were fitted with top canopies but these will be listed in the next volume, as will any conversions.

359046 taken at Nunhead, South East London in February 1981. This lot 3882 illustrates the normal condition of this class. Four years old, the condition is scruffy, caused chiefly by equipment pressing on the sides when being loaded and unloaded. (Author's Ref No W8955/DL)

365129 taken at Worksop, Nottinghamshire in February 1981. By contrast, this is an almost new lot 3978 wagon. It is believed that all these last three batches had flame red framing rather than the original freight brown. Certainly they had white lettering on black panels. (Author's Ref No W8963/DL)

Air-braked General Coal Hopper Wagons (HBA, HEA)

As a replacement for the HTV class on more general coal traffic, a new design was developed in the mid-1970s. Normal hopper bodywork of a clean, smooth design was fitted with the usual end supports and lower side struts. Brakegear was just air-braked and the bulk of the fleet was built with BR long-link suspension and thick springs; there were changes as noted below. Building details were as follows:

360000	32.5T HOPPER (HB 001A)	7/1975	3881	BR (Shildon)
360001 to 361998	32.5T HOPPER (HB 001B)	9/1976 to 3/1979	3885	BR (Shildon)

There were a number of anomalies. Early vehicles (up to 360226 at least) had end ladders above the coupling; this was obviously awkward and subsequent vehicles had the ladder moved to the left of the buffer beam. The prototype presumably had a centre ladder as well. Certain wagons had experimental suspension (360955 had Gloucester floating-axle suspension, 361784 to 86 had normal Brunninghaus suspension and 361798/9 had vertical Brunninghaus suspension). Subsequently virtually the whole fleet was given normal Brunninghaus suspension but this data, livery changes and conversions will be dealt with in the next volume.

360040 taken at Birkenhead Docks in November 1979. The HBA fleet was delivered in freight brown livery with no symbols. Many were used on industrial coal traffic, as seen with imported coal to Hawarden Bridge steel works. (Author's Ref No W8681/DL)

360630 taken at Hoo Junction, Rochester in November 1977. The repositioned end ladder is seen well in this view. The HBA wagons seen here were stored pending traffic and could be used as oil train barrier wagons if necessary. (Author's Ref No W6762/DL)

360879 taken at Maidstone, Kent in October 1977. The wagon seen here formed part of a Railfreight exhibition train which toured the country in 1977 seeking business. The livery remained freight brown but the new symbol was applied. (Author's Ref No W8692/DL)

361785 taken at Birkenhead Docks in November 1979. Also in Hawarden Bridge imported coal traffic, this wagon is one of the examples with Brunninghaus suspension. Still coded HBA at this time, such wagons later became coded HEA. (Author's Ref No W8699/DL)

361798 taken at Nunhead, South East London in April 1981. This experimental wagon was rather different. It has an uncommon form of Brunninghaus suspension and, painted orange with white lettering on black panels, is being used for comparison in a private-owner aggregate hopper train. (Author's Ref No W8988A/DL)

Air-braked 4-wheeled Steel-carrying Wagons (SAA, SAB, SBA)

This design was effectively an air-braked Double Bolster wagon which had been preceded by a prototype wagon, B920500 (built in 1966 to diagram 1/455 by BR, Ashford Works, to lot 3569). This had suspension, brakegear and other differences and was air-braked and vacuum through-piped.

TDC920500 taken at Tiverton Junction in March 1983. Seen here coded ZSB and in use as a barrier wagon, it is not known why or when the vertical boarding was fitted but it is in essentially original condition with the fold-up side stanchions of the production batch. (Author's Ref No W12940/DL)

Only one batch of production vehicles was built but it was complicated and rather ill-fated. Building details are below:

400000 to 400299	32T FLAT (STEEL AB)	12/1970 to 7/1971	3728 BR (Ashford)

Ostensibly 400000 to 400249 were built to diagram 1/440 and were supposedly all air-braked only. 400250 to 400299 were built to diagram 1/453 and were supposedly air-braked and vacuum through-piped. However, photographic evidence appears to reveal that, of the diagram 1/440 wagons, 400000 to 400045 were air-braked and vacuum through-piped and 400046 to 400199 were air-braked; this group were given the pre-TOPS code of STEEL AB. The diagram 1/453 wagons 400250 to 400299 were all air-braked but had minor stanchion differences and were given the pre-TOPS code of STEEL ABB. Revised diagrams were eventually issued in 1971.

This caused extreme confusion when TOPS codes were issued but eventually 400000 to 400045 became SAB, 400046 to 400249 became SAA, and 400250 to 400299 became SBA.

400045 taken at Hoo Junction, Rochester in January 1971. This brand-new STEEL AB wagon, in use as an oil train barrier wagon, clearly shows exactly what brake pipes were carried. The rough appearance of the sides is due to the fact that certain planks could be turned up to form low bolsters. (Author's Ref No W3091/DL)

400015 taken at Hoo Junction, Rochester in March 1982. This wagon carries the correct SAB code and has had the ends removed. It is probably in use as a runner wagon and was eventually recoded RRB. (Author's Ref No 10240/DL)

400093 taken at Battersea, South West London in August 1978. A very regular use in the late 1970s period was the transit of export tractors from Doncaster to Sheerness, Kent. This wagon, coded STEEL AB, contains red tractors. (Author's Ref No W7651/DL)

400216 taken at Battersea, London South West in March 1978. The other common tractor colour was sand yellow and a whole load of such vehicles is seen here. The wagon is correctly coded SAA. (Author's Ref No W7376/DL)

Air-braked 4-wheel Steel-carrying Wagons (SPA)

This class was the air-braked Plate wagon and, perhaps due to the large numbers of relatively modern SPV wagons, it was a fairly late addition to the air-braked fleet.

Two SAA wagons, numbered 460000 (ex-400100) and 460001 (ex-400142), were converted in May 1977 as design code SP 019A by BR (Ashford) to lot 3914. New four-part drop sides and fixed ends were provided but suspension and brakegear remained the same. These were followed in 1979 by two production batches. These differed by having only three-part drop sides and the latest brakegear and Brunninghaus suspension. Building details were as follows:

460002 to 460601	31T PLATE (SP 020A)	6/1979 to 2/1980	3839 BR (Shildon)
460602 to 461101	31T PLATE (SP 020A)	5/1980 to 2/1981	3962 BR (Shildon)

It must have been obvious fairly quickly that there was no lasting need for plate wagons as such. No fewer than three batches were cancelled (461102 to 461501 (lot 3962), 461502 to 461601 (lot 3995) and 461602 to 461701 (lot 3988)) and, as the photographs on the next page show, those in service were frequently used for other loads.

Many were converted or transferred to the civil engineers department and this will be covered in the next volume.

460000 taken at Maidstone, Kent in October 1977. Seen here in an exhibition train, the first prototype SPA is in maroon livery with all appropriate symbols. (Author's Ref No W7756/DL)

460002 taken at Cardiff, Tidal Sidings in September 1982. The production run of this class appeared in the flame red livery period and this was the only livery carried in general traffic by the basic SPA. Early vehicles, up to 460034, carried the symbols on the right. (Author's Ref No W11770/DL)

460330 taken at Hoo Junction, Rochester in October 1981. The more usual arrangement of symbols is seen on this lot 3839 wagon. The load is interesting and rather crudely tied down. (Author's Ref No W9070/DL)

460902 taken at Toton Yard, Nottinghamshire in February 1983. No ropes can be seen holding the Army trailers; presumably they were braked and secured internally. (Author's Ref No W12620/DL)

460505 taken at Hoo Junction, Rochester in December 1988. Increasingly, as vacuum-braked stock was withdrawn, SPA wagons began to be seen carrying wire coil on the traditional routes, in this case from Sheerness steel works. This lot 3839 vehicle has interesting symbol variations. (Author's Ref No W14386/DL)

Air-braked Flask Wagons (XKA, XKB)

Nuclear flask traffic began to increase during the period covered by this book, carrying waste from the various nuclear power stations. Sensitivity to this traffic also increased and vehicles built in the 1970s with little to disguise what was being carried were subsequently rebuilt. New vehicles built were as follows:

550000 to 550005	50T XKB FLASK (diagram 2/534)	1/1970 to 4/1970	3697 BR (Shildon)
550009 to 550014	50T XKB FLASK (XK 002A)	11/1976 to 1/1977	3886 BR (Ashford)
550015 to 550016	50T XKB FLASK (XK 003A)	11/1978 to 12/1978	3928 BR (Ashford)

(Note: Numbers 550006 to 550008 were issued to an obscure conversion on ex WD WWII 6-wheeled bogie Warwell wagons which, in fact, carried European RIV numbers.)

To the above were added B900509 to B900532, which were given new 4-wheeled bogies and air brakes and vacuum through-pipes. All these and the lot 3697 wagons had been withdrawn by 1991. The others had been modified expensively and will be covered in the next volume. During the review period, specific runner wagons did not appear to have been allocated. Conversions of these will also be covered in the next volume.

550000 taken at Trawsfynydd, North Wales in April 1971. Seen at a flask-loading terminal, this represents the new era of such wagons with the first lot 3697 vehicle. Livery was freight brown with black bogies and a white heat shield. Tare weight: 24-13. (Author's Ref No W3413/DL)

550004 taken at Warrington (Arpley) in February 1982. This view is of another lot 3697 wagon. Now rather weathered, presumably the flask is empty as the heat shield is not in use. Livery was an unusual pale blue with white livery. (Author's Ref No W11016/DL)

B900513 taken at Warrington (Arpley) in February 1982. Seen on the occasion as the above vehicle, this former vacuum-braked vehicle has been modified with changed braking and new Y25C bogies. Livery was black. (Author's Ref No W11017/DL)

550012 taken at Shildon Works. This view of a lot 3886 wagon shows it undergoing conversion that would hide the load under a sliding cover. The new additions can be plainly seen. The bodywork is a buff colour but the extensions are unpainted. (Author's Ref No W10015/DL)

Air-braked Bogie Steel-carrying Wagons (BAA, BAB)

This was the first bogie steel-carrying design to appear in the air-braked fleet and was a totally new design. It was rather short, resembling the Bogie Bolster E class, but much stronger and able to carry a heavier load. Fish-belly girder solebars were used and there was no separate bodywork, the load going straight onto the steel cross bracing. Tall ends were provided and stanchions slotted straight into the floor ends. Modern Y25C bogies were fitted. Building details were as follows:

900000 to 900048	100T FLAT (diagram 1/441)	9/1972 to 12/1972	3792	BR (Ashford)
900049 to 900124	100T FLAT (BA 001B)	12/1972 to 7/1973	3803	BR (Ashford)
900125 to 900198	100T FLAT (BA 001B)	8/1973 to 12/1973	3805	BR (Ashford)
900200 to 900273	100T FLAT (BA 001C)	11/1975 to 12/1975	3858	BR (Ashford)
900274 to 900305	100T FLAT (BA 002A)	11/1975 to 1/1976	3860	BR (Ashford)

900199 (lot 3805) and 900306 to 900390 (lot 3870) were cancelled.

900000 to 900048 (lot 3792) were air-braked and vacuum through-piped. They carried the code BOGIE STEEL AB and became BAB in due course. All the others were air-braked and were delivered as code BAA.

Very early in the career of this class, some vehicles were semi-permanently converted to carry strip coil cradles, as shown in the photographs. This was not formalised until the end of the review period and will be covered in detail in the next volume. The following wagons were known to have operated as coil wagons and may have been recoded on the wagon:

BKA: 900056-63/5-8/77/80/90/6/7, 900107-14/6-24/50/5/72/93/7, 900203/13/9/23/6/8/41/2/5/69/83/90/5, 900303.
BKB: 900001/6/9/12-4/9.

900016 taken at Tees Yard, Middlesbrough in April 1981. Establishment of what the original wagons looked like is a bit difficult due to coil-carrying modifications. This lot 3792 wagon, in freight brown livery with correct BAB code, is thought to be original. (Author's Ref No W9077/DL)

900152 taken at Severn Tunnel Junction in November 1975. This is the original lot 3805 design and the ends appear to be lower than the lot 3792 wagon opposite. Livery is freight brown with black bogies. (Author's Ref No W5705/DL)

900067 taken at Tees Yard, Middlesbrough in April 1981. One way of carrying strip coil on these vehicles was to use the so-called "kinky beam", which was bolted longitudinally to the floor. The load, usually sheeted, was loaded over the bogies. Code was BKA. (Author's Ref No W9078/DL)

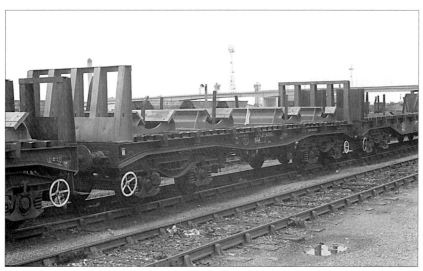

900103 taken at Tees Yard, Middlesbrough in April 1981. The second way of carrying strip coil was to fit transverse cradles, as seen here. This vehicle does not appear in the list opposite and retains the BAA code. Ends and cradles are flame red and solebar and bogies are black. (Author's Ref No W9079/DL)

Air-braked Bogie Steel-carrying Wagons (BBA)

The next bogie steel-carrying wagon design to appear was the BBA. This was a longer version of the BOGIE STEEL AB (BAA) design and had deeper solebars. Y25C bogies were fitted, the final batch (lot 3959) differing by having disc hand wheels on the bogies to operate the hand brakes. Livery was freight brown, with again the exception of the last batch, which was flame red with black solebar and bogies. Building details were as follows:

910000	100T FLAT (BB 001A)	1/1973	3845	BR (Shildon)
910001 to 910120	100T FLAT (BB 001C)	5/1975 to 1/1976	3857	BR (Ashford)
910161 to 910365	100T FLAT (BB 001C)	4/1977 to 11/1977	3872	BR (Ashford)
910367 to 910491	100T FLAT (BB 001B)	11/1976 to 4/1977	3871	BR (Ashford)
910492 to 910591	100T FLAT (BB 001F)	12/1979 to 10/1981	3959	BR (Ashford)

910366 became 920000, the prototype BLA (see page 77). B910121 to 910160 (lot 3871) and 910592 to 910691 (lot 3959) were cancelled.

910003/6, 910112/70/5, 910216/23/34/5/58/64/9/75/92, 910413/21-8/40/1/7/50/61/5/9/84/9 were converted to carry six strip coil cradles fixed to the floor transversely, the ends also being removed; there were no other conversions. Strip coil was also carried in "eye-to-sky" fashion as a regular load by ordinary BBA wagons, another such load being long steel billets.

910042 taken at Ashford Works in August 1975. This view shows to advantage the floor on both this class and the smaller BAA class. The wagons seen here would all have been lot 3857. (Author's Ref No W5111/DL)

910343 taken at Birkenhead Docks in February 1980. This wagon has seen about two years service and is reasonably weathered. The recording of quite a few such BBA wagons at this location suggests that steel was exported from here. (Author's Ref No W8837/DL)

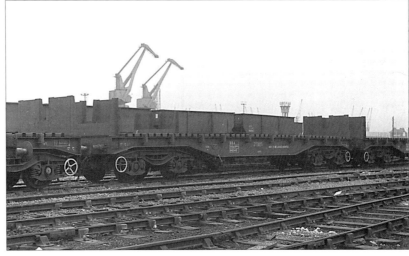

910498 taken at Fratton Yard, Portsmouth in February 1980. This wagon is fairly new and shows off the solid hand wheel that replaced the spoked version on lot 3959 vehicles. (Author's Ref No W8840B/DL)

910582 taken at Nunhead, South East London in September 1981. After about 910536, lot 3959 wagons have prominent lifting eyes above each bogie and this feature can be seen here. It was presumably a maintenance aid. (Author's Ref No W9096/DL)

910427 taken at Tees Yard, Middlesbrough in April 1981. This wagon is one of the only conversions of the BBA class and must have been carried out circa 1979, judging by the condition of this example. (Author's Ref No W9092/DL)

Air-braked Bogie Steel-carrying Wagons (BDA)

This was the third bogie steel-carrying wagon to appear in the fleet in that it was a conversion of traditional unfitted stock, in this case the 42T Bogie Bolster D wagon built during the 1950s. A prototype was converted in 1975 and was followed by production batches. The bodywork was not greatly altered and Y25C bogies were fitted. Lots 3888, 3907 and 3925 had lever-operated hand brakes and lots 3965 and 3968 had solid disc handbrake wheels in the centre of the bogies. Building details were as follows:

950000	80T BOLSTER (BD 006B)	10/1975	3888	BR (Swindon)
950001 to 950200	80T BOLSTER (BD 006C)	10/1977 to 8/1978	3907	BR (Ashford)
950201 to 950800	80T BOLSTER (BD 006C)	7/1978 to 9/1979	3925	BR (Ashford)
950801 to 950900	80T BOLSTER (BD 006D)	9/1979 to 12/1979	3965	BR (Shildon)
950901 to 951250	80T BOLSTER (BD 006D)	3/1980 to 3/1981	3968	BR (Shildon)

951251 to 951550 (lot 3968) were cancelled. Vehicles up to approximately 950799 were delivered in freight brown livery, although many were later repainted. From 950800 (that is, the last from lot 3925), the livery was flame red. There were a number of later conversions and these will be dealt with in the next volume.

950000 taken at Scunthorpe, Lincolnshire in February 1978. The prototype BDA wagon actually carried the lettering D BOLSTER BDA (PROTOTYPE) and is seen here in company with the BCA and KOA prototypes. (Author's Ref No W7305/DL)

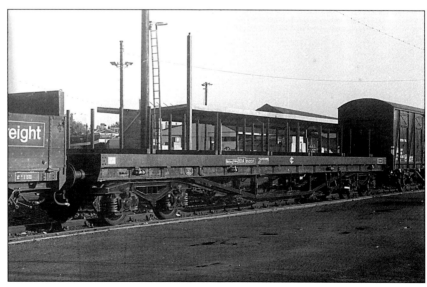

950137 taken at Maidstone, Kent in October 1977. By contrast, this BDA was photographed in the exhibition train with the prototype SPA and others designs being publicised by BR at the time. (Author's Ref No W7547/DL)

950565 taken at Scunthorpe, Lincolnshire in February 1981. This lot 3925 wagon, and 950564 as well, have an experimental pattern of bogie which was later used on ballast hopper wagons. (Author's Ref No W9105/DL)

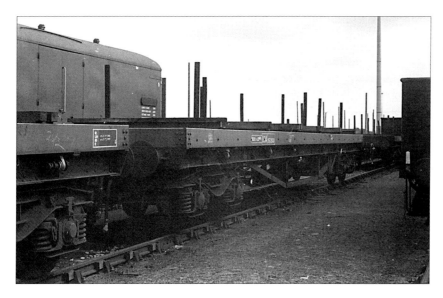

950800 taken at Hoo Junction, Rochester in April 1981. This lot 3925 wagon was the first BDA to be delivered in flame red livery, it being the last of lot 3925. (Author's Ref No W9109A/DL)

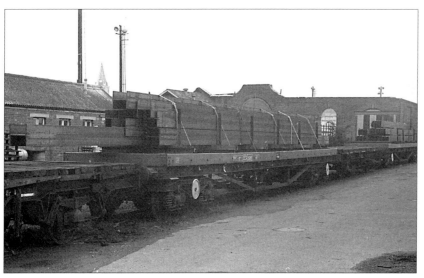

950811 taken at Rochester, Kent in May 1981. Flanked by two SAA wagons for the overhanging load of H Girders, this view of the BD 006D variant shows the disc handbrake wheels well. (Author's Ref No W911/DL)

Air-braked Bogie Steel-carrying Wagons (BPA, BRA, XVA)

After the BDA class had been successfully introduced, it was decided to also convert unfitted BOPLATE E wagons, vacuum-braked BORAIL wagons and unfitted TRESTLE ED wagons. All were produced in the red/black livery period and none lasted in original converted condition very long, the BPA and XVA wagons being converted to other duties and the BRA wagons passing to the civil engineers fleet, which they had in fact usually served anyway. Building details were as follows:

965000 to 965049	80T FLAT (BP 004A)	5/1980 to 7/1980	3985	BR (Shildon)
965050 to 965079	80T FLAT (BP 004A)	5/1981 to 6/1981	4011	BR (Shildon)
967500 to 967649	100T FLAT (BR 006A)	7/1981 to 1/1982	4012	BR (Shildon)
990000	80T STEEL (XV 005A)	5/1977	3911	BR (Ashford)
990001 to 990049	80T STEEL (XV 005A)	9/1979 to 12/1979	3961	BR (Shildon)

Right: 965030 taken at Scunthorpe, Lincolnshire in July 1980. Proof that the BPA class did actually carry the load they were designed for. Most changes from the original design were to the brakegear and bogies. (Author's Ref No W8879/DL)

Below: 965070 taken at Tees Yard, Middlesbrough in May 1981. With Middlesbrough's transporter bridge behind it, this lot 4011 wagon has just been delivered from Shildon works. There are no apparent differences between batches. (Author's Ref No W9121/DL)

967554 taken at Burton-upon-Trent in September 1982. The BRA class were provided for any large bulky steel loads but, in truth, they generally carried rail or, in this case, part of a point for the civil engineers. (Author's Ref No: W11885/DL)

990007 taken at Scunthorpe, Lincolnshire in July 1981. The load-retaining chains of the unfitted TRESTLE ED wagons were changed for blue nylon straps and these were also used on many other classes needing such fittings. (Author's Ref No W8881/DL)

990042 taken at Scunthorpe, Lincolnshire in July 1981. This high angle view of a loaded XVA wagon shows that vehicles from the air braked fleet did mix with other stock in suitable yards and were probably moved together in short local trains. (Author's Ref No W8884/DL)

Air-braked Miscellaneous Types (BCA, BLA, FMA, KOA, KTA)

Certain small classes are listed here.

920000	100T FLAT (BL 001A)	4/1976	3896	BR (Ashford)
960000 to 960001	60T BOLSTER (BC 008A)	1/1976	3889	BR (Swindon)
150000 to 150001	10T CAR (FZA) (Outer)	7/1970	3713	BR (Ashford)
150002 to 150004	10T CAR (FZA) (Inner)	7/1970	3714	BR (Ashford)
699000 to 699001	LOWLINER A SET	10/1971	3729	BR (Ashford)
699002 to 699003	LOWLINER B SET	1/1972	3730	BR (Ashford)

The BLA wagon was a one-off experimental wagon based on BBA 910366. It was not a success and passed to the civil engineers fleet by 1980 when it was given a vacuum through-pipe.

920000 taken at Battersea, South West London in August 1979. Seen at Stewarts Lane Works, this vehicle, painted in freight brown was probably waiting to enter the workshops to have the modifications made for civil engineers use. It became YNB GOLDFISH. (Author's Ref No W7752/DL)

The BCA class was not proceeded with, there probably being enough BDA wagons available. In due course, suitable BCV wagons were given air through-pipes to become BCW; these will be covered in the next volume.

960000 taken at Scunthorpe, Lincolnshire in February 1978. The two BCA prototypes ended up with the CM&EE department and were coded YVA. Livery seen here is freight brown and the lettering is PROTOTYPE BCA. (Author's Ref No W7309/DL)

The FZA class was, in fact, a five-wagon low-loading two-axle car-carrying set which seems to have met with early withdrawal. They may have been replaced by three-wagon FMA sets. These were two outer Freightliner wagons fitted with end ramps and one inner Freightliner wagon between them. Known sets were as follows:

601009-602003-601010; 601011-602022-601015; 602031-602067-602083
(Note: Some inner vehicles must have had buffer beams, as the remaining wagons, in numerical order, are: 602007/9/10/7/23/45/60/71.)

The BLA wagon was a one-off experimental wagon based on BBA 910366. It was not a success and passed to the civil engineers fleet by 1980 when it was given a vacuum through-pipe.

601009-602003-601010 taken at Battersea, South West London in August 1977. Loaded with red International tractors built at Doncaster and bound for Sheerness, Kent, this FMA set makes an impressive sight. The other vehicles were SAA 4-wheeled steel-carrying wagons. (Author's Ref No W7075/DL)

Unidentified FMA set taken at Southampton in August 1979. A different load is seen here with Leyland truck chassis from Eastleigh. Unlike the tractors, they can only be loaded on the flat, as loading on the ramp would mean too high a load. (Author's Ref No W10932A/DL)

The height of the ISO container has always caused problems over lines in the UK which have low bridges and tunnels. The Lowliner class were an attempt to provide a service in these parts of the country. The Lowliner A had 4-wheeled bogies and the Lowliner B had 6-wheeled bogies but the bodywork was essentially the same. Neither set was being used when photographed.

699000-699001 taken at Temple Mills Yard, East London in August 1979. The skeletal nature of the framework can be seen in this high angle view. Once loaded with containers the whole set would be more substantial. (Author's Ref No W7789A/DL)

699002-699003 taken at Doncaster, South Yorkshire in February 1981. The LOWLINER B appears to a rather longer set altogether. Interestingly, private owner wagons are now doing the job these wagons were built for. (Author's Ref No W10925A/DL)

Finally in this section, some conversions in the early years of the SAA class need to be looked at. Apart from the ones that became the prototype SPA wagons, 400004 and 400181 became 4-wheeled nuclear waste wagons for which I have no photographs; these were later sold to British Nuclear Fuels Ltd.

400049 and 400054 became KOA wire coil wagons and are illustrated overleaf. 400038 became an FPB coal container wagon and will be dealt with in the next volume.

400057/64-6/91/6, 400103/13/5/21/9/30/5/7/9/43/8/59/68/88, 400200/3/11/4/7/8/24/7/8/33/8 /40/4/6/50/2-4/6/64/75/89 operated as KTA strip coil wagons until 1983, when they became RRA.

Finally, 400105 and 400267 have both been recorded with modifications for unknown purposes.

400049 taken at Scunthorpe, Lincolnshire in February 1978. The bodywork was very much the standard wire coil type operating from Scunthorpe but the two ex-SAA conversions probably had a chassis with inferior running, as standard SPA wagons were later converted. (Author's Ref No W7306/DL)

400267 taken at Doncaster, South Yorkshire in August 1980. It is thought that this conversion was probably associated with the export tractor traffic, which used this class of vehicle. (Author's Ref No W8789/DL)

400065 taken at Ebbw Vale, South Wales in November 1975. This is one of the wagons listed as being converted to KTA. There is no sign of the usual floor spigots that such vehicles had, but the box at one end of this vehicle and the one to the left may be part of an earlier conversion. (Author's Ref No W5758/DL)

Air-braked Miscellaneous Wagons (MFA and WR Test Train)

Two HBA coal hoppers were built as scrap metal wagons. Building details were as follows:

390000 to 390001	32.5T OPEN (MF 001A)	8/1976	3903 BR (Shildon)

At the time they were built, most scrap traffic was being carried in MCV and MXV wagons and although the higher bodywork allowed for a bigger load, they were incompatible with vacuum-braked trains. They soon passed into storage and were in the CM&EE fleet by 1983.

Right: ADC390000 taken at Basingstoke, Hampshire in March 1981. The body style was the one that was adopted for all four-wheeled scrap wagons after 1976, although none were as plain as this. Livery is freight brown with minimal changes to the lettering. (Author's Ref No W12971/DL)

Below: ADC390001 taken at Basingstoke, Hampshire in June 1983. The MFA concept might have worked if through vacuum-pipes had been fitted but, as it retains the original HBA suspension, it was obviously not thought to be worthwhile. (Author's Ref No W13090/DL)

For obscure reasons, the Western Region of BR decided to convert a test train of various vehicles to examine the operations of air-braked freight trains between Oxford and Worcester. The vehicles were converted in 1970 and, when the tests had been completed in 1972, the wagons became part of the general air-braked fleet.

The following types of vehicle were used:

13T ALL-STEEL HIGHFITS (OHB): B476462, B479731, B481274, B481866, B482804, B488985, B489405, E280264, E294336, E294639, E294913, E296740.

12T VANFITS (VVB): B778246, B778331, B780046, B780465, B780575, B781007, B781263, B781375, B781479, B781595, B786001, B786393.

12T PALVANFITS (VPB): B778971, B779026, B779834, B781763, B781847, B781864, B781875.

22T TUBE VB (STB): B730595, B731597, B732039, B733045.

22T PLATE VB (SPB): B934398, B935416, B935653, B935793, B936129.

The OHB Highfits operated on air-braked network services until about 1979. They were then transferred to the departmental fleet to carry spare parts and one at least (LDE294639) remained in service in 1992.

The VVB Vanfits and VPB Palvanfits may have operated similarly; I have only recorded B781854 in use in 1976. They appear to have remained in departmental stores use as late as 1989.

The STB Tube VB wagons were in use as RBB barrier wagons in 1978 and one (ADB731597) was in use as a wagon wheel carrier in 1992.

The SPB Plate VB wagons were converted to FPB coal container wagons and were in use as such in 1984. One (DB935416) was recorded in 1992 as a Bream civil engineers runner wagon.

E294639 taken at Brixton, South East London in June 1979. Carrying what look like grey naval stores crates, two OHB wagons are seen in a mixed air brake network train. Livery is probably rusty bauxite with new codes and a faded ABN symbol. (Author's Ref No W7784/DL)

E296740 taken at Toton Yard, Nottinghamshire in September 1978. With the grey sheet covering the details, only the suspension and partially obscured ABN disc reveal this to be an OHB wagon. (Author's Ref No W7162/DL)

ADB778246 taken at Dover, Kent in April 1981. A conscious effort was made by BR authorities in the early 1980s to locate these air-braked conversions and transfer them to carry urgent stores and wagon parts. This van is freshly repainted in olive green livery. (Author's Ref No W9951/DL)

ADB781007 taken at Brixton, South East London in April 1980. Once transferred, these vehicles operated in a mixed air brake network train. This example, in olive green, is seen marshalled between an OBA and an SAA carrying tractors. (Author's Ref No W9952/DL)

B781854 taken at Falkirk, Scotland in April 1976. In view of the poor riding characteristic of these vans, perhaps the long-link suspension improved this. Livery is bauxite. No code is visible and the significance of the white diamond symbol is not known. (Author's Ref No W5518/DL)

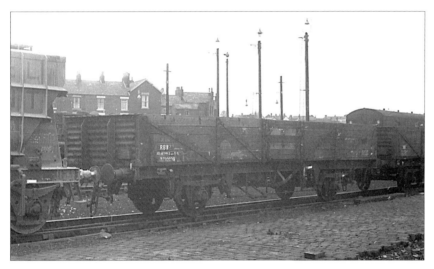

B732039 taken at Chester Wagon Works in February 1979. The clarity of the RBB code when compared with the other lettering suggests recent transfer to barrier wagon use. Livery is dirty bauxite with new codes and a faded ABN symbol. (Author's Ref No W8773/DL)

B935653 taken at Mossend Yard, Scotland in March 1984. To carry coal containers, the original sides and floor were removed and locating spigots welded onto the side of the solebar. Most but not all retained the original ends. Livery was grime. (Author's Ref No W13800/DL)

Conflat Conversions on Boplate E Wagons

These conversions are part of the traditional fleet but, as most of them were later fitted with air through-pipes, they have been left until last.

Conflat E (FEV/FEW)

These vehicles were converted circa 1969/70 to carry three BD-sized containers between Paddington and the West of England. Subsequently, they carried steel containers in South Wales. Numbers were as follows:

B947862/74/93, B947900/12/3/26/32/4/6/7/52/69/70/2/3/5/7/90/3/8, B948000-3/5.

B947998 taken at Margam Yard, South Wales in March 1983. The containers here are unloaded and were probably sheeted in transit. The working was probably only a short one. (Author's Ref No W12805/DL)

Conflat EE (FEV/FEW)

These vehicles appear to have been additional to the Conflat Condor fleet covered in the previous volume of this series. Numbers were as follows:
B947860/71/6/9/90, B947906/16/261/33/50/60/83, B948007.

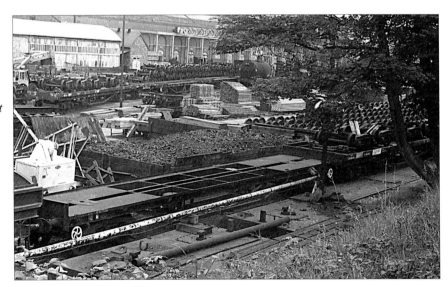

B947906 taken at Ashford Works, Kent in October 1978. The vehicle shown here is thought to be out of use and awaiting conversion to a match/barrier wagon for use at Ashford. (Author's Ref No W7079/DL)

Conflat Clay (FEV/FEW)

These vehicles were converted circa 1970 to carry two ISO-sized containers for china clay between Fowey and the Avonmouth Docks. Numbers were as follows:

B947861/5/8/80/95, B947946/86.

B947880 taken at Avonmouth Docks, Somerset in February 1976. The containers seen here were orange and covered in translucent blue sheets for what was probably export traffic. This appears to have ceased by 1981. (Author's Ref No W5688/DL)

Conflat Coke (FEV/FEW)

These vehicles were converted circa 1969 to carry two ISO-sized containers for coke between Wakefield and Derwenthaugh Coke Works, Tyneside. Subsequently, the containers were given top covers and the vehicles became FEW. They were still regular use in 1983. Numbers were as follows:

B947883/7/91/6, B947905/10/9/20/3/8/30/43/58/64/6/92, B948045/85/97, B948130/98, B948200/12/27/52/53/68, B948358/62, B948405.

B947883 taken at Wakefield, West Yorkshire in February 1979. The containers were generally dirty but were grey with a white name. Retention of the original ends varied. (Author's Ref No W9163/DL)

B948405 taken at Wakefield, West Yorkshire in July 1980. As mentioned on the previous caption, retention of the original ends varied and it has not been retained in this case. Two bogie variations were found on these, this being the roller bearing plate bogie. (Author's Ref No W9180/DL)

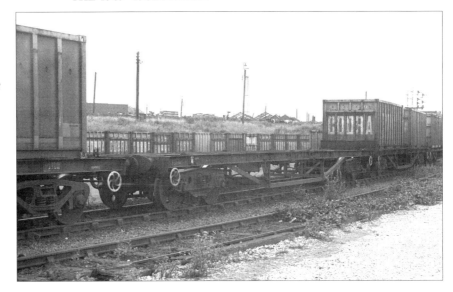

Summary of Period 1st January 1969 to 31st December 1982

As far as the "traditional" fleet was involved, BR appeared to waste a lot of money on rebuilding mineral wagons that had only a comparatively short life in revenue earning traffic. This may have been for political reasons to offset hardship over workshop closures.

Other "traditional" designs were converted to cater for new traffic needs and this was a more sensible exercise.

The air-braked fleet progressed along expected lines, although with hindsight possibly too many general merchandise types were constructed. Certainly the provision of new Plate wagons and Boplate wagons, to say nothing of Trestles and Borails, seems to have been a bit excessive.

400105 taken at York, Dringhouses in February 1979. Many attempts were made to find a permanent use for the rather accident-prone Steel AB. This conversion is not documented but may have been intended to carry narrow pipes. (Author's Ref No W7778/DL)

In the next volume, we will see that the "traditional" fleet basically marked time with only changes to codes and the addition of air-pipes.

The air-braked fleet saw the introduction of some new types at the same time as the transfer of many older vehicles to the departmental fleets.

Many types were either updated with the latest suspension or totally rebuilt for new use.

We will also cover the new Railfreight livery, including the experiments, and the train load freight "sector" livery. This will take the story up to Privatisation and the disposition of the stock to the three new companies, Loadhaul, Mainline and Transrail.

The fortunes of these and their merging into EWS is another story, and will be left to others to cover.

TDB931631 taken at Grays, Essex in October 1980. The air-piping of certain wagons had started back in the late 1960s with the transference of unfitted 22T Plate wagons to become oil train barrier wagons. Many of these were still in use into the 1980s and only the lettering indicated that they were not ordinary Plate wagons. (Author's Ref No W10035/DL)